LOCAL INCOME TAXES:
Economic Effects and Equity

D1310818

Local
Income Taxes:
ECONOMIC EFFECTS
AND EQUITY

by
R. STAFFORD SMITH
Faculty of Business Administration and Commerce
The University of Alberta, Canada

INSTITUTE OF GOVERNMENTAL STUDIES
University of California, Berkeley 1972

721826

Library of Congress Cataloging in Publication Data

Smith, R   Stafford.
   Local income taxes.

   A revision of the author's thesis, University of
California, Berkeley.
   Bibliography: p. 205-220
   1. Income tax--San Francisco Co., Calif.
2. Taxation--San Francisco Co., Calif. I. Title.
HJ9205.S3S65 1972   336.2'4'0979461   77-633802
ISBN 0-87772-076-2

$4.50

To Bets

 **CONTENTS**

FIGURES

 **FOREWORD**

Students of government are engaged in a seemingly never-ending search for equitable means to finance governmental services and facilities. Conversely they are on the lookout for ways of taxing the citizenry so as to produce the most revenue, while doing the least harm to the polity and the economy.

Recent developments in California and elsewhere have combined massive increases in demand for governmental services in metropolitan areas with turtle-like sluggishness at the state level in pushing ahead with tax reform. The pressures are growing, year by year. Soon a breakthrough must come.

Meanwhile the more we can learn about alternatives at either the state or local levels, the better. R. Stafford Smith has examined one of the more promising possibilities, the local income tax, basing his exhaustive analysis on a case study of the City and County of San Francisco. His study is a logical companion and sequel to two other Institute publications: *Agenda for Local Tax Reform*, by George F. Break (1970), and *Neighborhood Distribution of Local Public Services*, by Charles S. Benson and Peter B. Lund (1969). These also considered where the money comes from and what it is spent for, respectively, with special attention to socioeconomic effects and issues of equity.

A careful reading of Smith's work makes it clear that the local income tax can provide significant relief

from the burdensome property tax. But most local income
taxes, being levied at a flat rate or otherwise having
low progressivity, have had limited success in improving the equity of the local tax structure. In sum, the
local income tax may be very helpful in many areas, but
it falls short of the fundamental and across-the-board
reform demanded by the existing state-local tax structure.

Nevertheless, Smith's well-documented findings
about the local income tax, both positive and negative,
should provide helpful guidance to future fiscal policymakers. His realistic evaluation may also recommend a
more cautious view to income-tax enthusiasts, some of
whom have seen the source as a revenue panacea, or have
hoped that through it the central city can "sock the
suburbs." Moreover, local income taxes may begin to
look much more desirable to many other policymakers if
general tax reform is postponed much longer, because
pressure to find workable alternatives to the property
tax is becoming more intense. In any case, this careful work of R. Stafford Smith will prove useful.

The Institute owes special thanks to Mary Fitch,
whose editorial capabilities helped transform a doctoral
dissertation into a readable public policy document.
Harriet Nathan, Institute Editor, also assisted and pre-
sided over the process, and Katherine Castro of the Institute's clerical staff prepared the final pages with
care and skill.

Stanley Scott
Assistant Director

 **PREFACE**

Throughout the United States, cities have experienced a rapidly rising demand for public expenditures. In the search for revenues to finance these expenditures, local governments must consider all possible forms of taxation, among them income taxes. By 1968, some form of income taxation was already employed by local governments with jurisdiction over more than 19 million people. Large cities employing local income taxes included New York, Philadelphia, Detroit, Baltimore, Cleveland and St. Louis. However, the widespread adoption of local income taxes has been accompanied by little analysis of their economic effects.

This study provides a further look at the economic effects of local income taxes, and in particular, an examination of the probable effects of local income taxes on the City and County of San Francisco. When the study began in the fall of 1967, a state law requiring uniform assessment ratios for all types of taxable property had just eliminated the preferential treatment previously received by San Francisco residential property owners. In most cases, this change had raised residential property taxes from 50 to 100 percent within one year. The resulting pressure on property taxes had stimulated a search for alternative tax forms capable of raising large amounts of revenue. A local income tax was one such source briefly considered by the mayor and his advisors.

Although one can only speculate, it seems likely that local income taxes would have received more serious consideration if more information had been available concerning their revenue-raising ability and their economic effects. This study attempts to provide such information as a basis for future policy decisions. The theoretical conclusions concerning the economic effects of local income taxes are also applicable to other cities. And although San Francisco data are used most extensively, the methodology developed should provide a guide for others wishing to examine the effects of local income taxes.

It is vital that policymakers have answers to important tax questions before making their policy decisions. The first questions most legislators would ask relate to how well the tax has performed in other jurisdictions. How much revenue is this form of taxation capable of raising? Should more than one form be considered? If more than one exists, which appears most desirable? Chapter I deals with each of these questions in an attempt to persuade the legislator that it is worth pursuing the analysis of local income taxation offered in this study.

But since the study must be of finite length, several issues relevant to any form of taxation cannot be considered in detail. In order to assure the reader that the author recognizes the importance of these issues, they are dealt with briefly in Chapter II. The points examined include the administrative and compliance costs of local income taxes and the effects of income taxation on the location decisions made by businesses. The chapter concludes that none of the issues considered offers sufficient reason to cease the investigation of local income taxes.

The succeeding chapters deal with the main question of this study:

When a local income tax is levied and the revenues result in an immediate reduction in property tax rates so that municipal revenues remain unchanged, what will be the economic effects?

The general impact of this tax change on the allocation of resources is examined theoretically in Chapter III, while the remaining chapters attempt to measure empirically the effects of local income taxation on the distribution of wealth and income among residents. A distinction is made between renters and homeowners; business-tax shifting is considered; and the extent and effects of tax capitalization are examined.

Chapter IV measures the effects of the tax change on the disposable income of various income classes. Effects on renters and on homeowners are calculated separately. The effect of such a tax change on the vertical equity of the tax structure is also examined. Since the substitution of income taxes for property taxes frequently reduces the share of local taxes paid by business, Chapter V considers the effect of such a reduction on the distribution of income within the community. In Chapter VI, the phenomenon of tax capitalization in San Francisco is examined. The relationship of the tax change to capitalization and the distribution of wealth is considered. In Chapter VII, the contribution non-residents make to central city revenues is examined in relation to the services the city provides to them. Findings are summarized in Chapter VIII, and conclusions presented.

Collection and analysis of data for this monograph took place from the fall of 1967 to the spring of 1969. During that time I was writing my Ph.D. dissertation for the Department of Economics at the University of California, Berkeley.

This study has benefited from the assistance of many individuals. I am indebted to the numerous employees of the San Francisco Assessor's and Controller's Offices and to Mr. Fred Martin of the Greater San Francisco Chamber of Commerce. All gave freely of their time and provided valuable information. Thomas Cowing, now of the State University of New York, Binghamton, provided valuable suggestions concerning the treatment of the material in Chapter VI. And I am particularly grateful to my wife,

Libby, for her useful comments on the various drafts, her help at the typewriter, and her continual encouragement.

My greatest debts are to Professors Eugene C. Lee, George F. Break and Malcolm M. Davisson of the University of California. Professors Lee and Break provided valuable guidance through each stage of this study. As my Ph.D. dissertation advisor, Professor Davisson planted the seed from which this study grew, carefully read the various drafts, and provided constant and much appreciated encouragement.

I, of course, remain fully responsible for any errors and shortcomings.

R. Stafford Smith

An Examination of Existing Local Income Taxes

THE EXTENT OF LOCAL INCOME TAXES

By the end of 1968, local governments in the United States were levying income taxes on a large portion of the American people. Twenty-two major cities, with a total population of more than 18 million, were employing this form of local taxation,[1] while another 150 cities with populations in excess of 10,000 relied on similar taxes. Detroit, Kansas City, Baltimore, New York City and Cleveland enacted income tax ordinances within the past decade, and similar taxes have been under consideration in Atlanta, Boston, Chicago, Dallas, Fort Worth, Los Angeles, Minneapolis and San Francisco. In Ohio over 5.5 million persons were covered by local income tax laws,[2] and in Pennsylvania, thousands of smaller local governmental units including cities, counties, school and special-purpose districts levied local income taxes. Between 1939 and 1968, the use of local income taxes increased significantly. Table I shows the lengthening list of cities with 1960 populations over 25,000 that had adopted the local tax by 1968.

THE REVENUE YIELD OF LOCAL INCOME TAXES

The ability of local income taxes to generate large amounts of revenue is beyond question. In 1967, a group of cities with more than 300,000 inhabitants raised 32.1 percent of their tax revenues through municipal income taxes. For some examples, see Table II. It indicates

1

the revenue-raising ability and per capita yield of local
income taxes for that year in the 11 largest cities
involved. Thus, Philadelphia raised $118.8 million and
Detroit $46.5 million; while local income taxes in New
York City, in their first year, raised $329.3 million.[3]
Per capita yield ranged from $19 in Kansas City to $58 in
Philadelphia.

Further, while Philadelphia and Pittsburgh raised
$129.7 million in local income tax revenues, the approxi-
mately 3000 smaller local Pennsylvania governments raised
an additional $125 million. Similarly, while the cities
of Columbus, Toledo and Cincinnati raised about $48.3
million, a group of 87 smaller municipalities in Ohio
raised sums totaling $72.7 million in amounts ranging
from Dayton's $14.3 million down to Navarre's $18,863.[4]
In 1965, per capita local income tax yield ranged from
$130 in St. Bernard to $6 in Hubbard, with $35 as the
average for the large cities of Cincinnati, Columbus,
Toledo and Dayton.[5]

THE USE OF LOCAL INCOME TAX REVENUES

While local income tax revenues have been used in
very different ways, most local income tax ordinances
assign revenues to general municipal operations. Canton,
Ohio, originally levied its local income tax to help
erect a new city hall, with the remaining revenues to be
used for general municipal operations. In Louisville,
Kentucky, the local occupational tax was initially levied
to raise funds for the servicing of bonded debt. But
since more was raised than was needed for this purpose,
revenues were diverted to the general fund and the special capital fund. Columbus, Ohio, and Gadsden, Alabama,
provided in their ordinances that income tax revenues
could be used for debt retirement and servicing as well
as for other general municipal operations.

In addition to providing general revenues to Pennsylvania cities, local income taxes are a source of
revenue for many Pennsylvania counties, school and

TABLE I

CITIES WITH 1960 POPULATIONS OVER 25,000
LEVYING LOCAL INCOME TAXES
(By date of tax adoption, 1939 to 1968)

Date and city	Date and city	Date and city
1939 Philadelphia, Pa.[3]	**1956** Gadsden, Ala.[1] Covington, Ky.[1] Wilkinsburg, Pa.	**1964** Kansas City, Mo.[2]
1946 Toledo, O.[2]		**1965** Flint, Mich.[2] Saginaw, Mich.[1] York, Pa.[1] Portsmouth, O.
1947 Columbus, O.[2]	**1957** Bethlehem, Pa.[1]	
1948 St. Louis, Mo.[3] Louisville, Ky.[2] Erie, Pa.[2] Scranton, Pa.[2] Altoona, Pa.[1] Johnstown, Pa.[1] Aliquippa Boro, Pa. New Castle, Pa. Sharon, Pa. Youngstown, O.[2] Springfield, O.[1]	**1958** Allentown, Pa.[2] Alliance, O. Middletown, O. **1959** Lancaster, Pa.[1] Easton, Pa. Lima, O.[1] Marion, O. Newark, O. Zanesville, O.	**1966** Baltimore, Md.[3] New York, N.Y.[3] Bowling Green, Ky. Highland Park, Mich. Chester, Pa.[1] Harrisburg, Pa.[1] Wilkes-Barre, Pa.[1] Cuyahoga Falls, O. Findlay, O.
1949 Dayton, O.[2]	**1960** Owensboro, Ky. Hamilton, O.[1] Mansfield, O. Massillon, O.	**1967** Grand Rapids, Mich.[2] Battle Creek, Mich. Cleveland, O.[3] Euclid, O.[1] Parma City, O.[1] East Cleveland, O. Garfield Heights, O. Maple Heights, O. Shaker Heights, O. South Euclid, O.
1952 Lexington, Ky.[1] Newport, Ky. Warren, O.[1]	**1961** West Mifflin Boro, Pa.	
1953 Williamsport, Pa.	**1962** Detroit, Mich.[3] Hamtramck, Mich. Akron, O.[2] Steubenville, O.	
1954 Pittsburgh, Pa.[3] Cincinnati, O.[3] Canton, O.[2] Barberton, O. Norwood, O.	**1963** McKeesport, Pa. Lancaster, O.	**1968** Lansing, Mich.[2] Cleveland Heights, O.[1] Kettering, O.[1]

[1] More than 50,000 but less than 100,000.

[2] 100,000 to 500,000.

[3] Over 500,000.

Source: Tax Foundation, Inc., *City Income Taxes* (New York: 1967), p. 23, and U.S., Advisory Commission on Intergovernmental Relations, *State and Local Finances, Significant Features, 1966 to 1969* (Washington, D.C.: 1968), pp. 95-97.

TABLE II

ELEVEN LARGEST CITIES USING LOCAL INCOME TAXES:
THE YIELD IN 1967

City	Income tax collections (millions)	Per capita income tax collections	Percentage of total city tax collections
New York City	$329.3	$41	13.5
Philadelphia	118.8	58	46.6
Detroit	46.5	29	30.1
Baltimore	24.8	27	13.9
St. Louis	28.8	42	34.1
Pittsburgh	10.9	20	20.8
Cincinnati	19.0	38	40.4
Kansas City, Mo.	10.6	19	24.3
Louisville	15.1	39	51.6
Columbus	17.5	31	72.3
Toledo	11.8	31	57.4

Source: U.S., Advisory Commission on Intergovernmental Relations [ACIR], State and Local Finances, Significant Features, 1966 to 1969 (Washington, D.C.: 1968), pp. 95-97.

special districts. At least two other areas have authorized the use of local income taxes for school districts: On February 1, 1966, Jefferson County, Kentucky, began collecting an occupational tax to help finance schools in the county; and in 1968, New Mexico passed legislation enabling counties to levy a surtax of up to 50 percent of the state income tax for school purposes.

MODEL LOCAL INCOME TAX PROPOSALS

Model local income tax ordinances in Ohio, Michigan and New York show substantial variation in scope and content. The 1958 Ohio ordinance was developed by the Ohio Municipal League in an attempt to facilitate uniform local income tax laws throughout the state, but because local income taxes already existed, the Municipal League had little flexibility in developing the ordinance.[6] Consequently, it contains neither taxation of unearned income nor allowance for deductions and exemptions. In contrast, Michigan's Uniform Local Income Tax Ordinance, which must be followed exactly by any Michigan city wishing to use a local income tax, spells out the income that is taxable, the exemptions and deductions to be allowed, and the liability of residents, nonresidents and businesses.[7] New York City's ordinances for the taxation of both personal and corporate income are even more detailed.[8]

Each of the above models serves different needs. The Ohio model recommends a form of local tax that simplifies collection and administration. The Michigan and New York City ordinances, while more difficult to administer, are clearly more equitable forms of local taxation, for they tax unearned as well as earned income and provide for deductions and exemptions.

COORDINATION OF TAX POLICIES WITHIN METROPOLITAN AREAS

The model uniform ordinances developed in Michigan and Ohio provide one means of increasing coordination of

tax policies in metropolitan areas, and reducing tax
competition and disputes concerning taxing authority.
Without uniform ordinances the problems of tax competition can be particularly acute in the larger metropolitan
areas, since it is possible for both business and labor
to locate in new communities and still have access to
the same markets. Independent enactment of local income
taxes by individual communities in a metropolitan area
would lead either to the adoption of less desirable forms
of local income taxes or to undesirable relocation
effects. Recognizing this, the U.S. Advisory Commission
on Intergovernmental Relations made several recommendations with regard to the enactment of local income taxes.

Recommendations of the U.S. Advisory
Commission on Intergovernmental Relations

In a January 1968 publication, the U.S. Advisory
Commission on Intergovernmental Relations (ACIR) made
three recommendations intended to further metropolitan
coordination of local income taxes, and by implication
to restrict local autonomy. First, for Standard Metropolitan Statistical Areas (SMSAs), the ACIR believed that
local income taxes should be imposed if and only if each
county governing board within the SMSA enacted an identical tax. (The county was chosen as the relevant unit
because it was likely to be the smallest governmental
unit encompassing an entire urban area.) If any county
opposed the tax, or wished to terminate its income tax,
the income tax would be repealed throughout the SMSA.
Second, the ACIR suggested that state laws ensure that
any county income tax would be administered by a state
tax collecting agency. Third, the ACIR recommended that
the local tax be levied as a percent of the state tax,
with the same rules and regulations applying to both
"except when, in the judgment of the [tax commissioner]
such rules would be inconsistent or not feasible of
proper administration."[9]

As the ACIR was no doubt aware, its recommendations
could be accepted only as a package. A local income tax,

for example, would be a wise supplement to the state
income tax only if an identical tax were applied
throughout the metropolitan area.

Progressive state income taxes make metropolitan
coordination of local supplements even more desirable.
To date, only Maryland municipalities have imposed such
a supplement: a 50 percent surtax on the state income
tax, with rates ranging from 1 to 2.5 percent. On
taxable income in excess of $3000, the local tax is 2.5
percent, the highest rate imposed by any local jurisdiction in the country. Yet as Table III indicates, 25
of the 38 states presently imposing state income taxes
have marginal rates exceeding Maryland's 5 percent; in
many cases, other state income taxes are more progressive
than Maryland's. In these states a local supplement
similar to Maryland's would work poorly.

If an income tax is to serve as an important source
of revenue for a city government, it appears that a supplement close to 50 percent would be required. Therefore, this study will focus on the effects of a 50
percent supplement to state income taxes. A supplement
under 50 percent would raise little revenue: In San
Francisco, even a 50 percent supplement would raise only
$23 million, less than a one percent levy on all income
earned in the city. Yet a 50 percent supplement would
create a sizable incentive to escape the tax, especially
for high-income families and businesses. Thus metropolitan cooperation in levying identical taxes becomes
imperative. In order to minimize relocation effects,
the metropolitan area must encompass a large territory.

Relocation Effects and Metropolitan Coordination

Although thousands of local jurisdictions currently
impose income taxes, there is no case in which state
legislation requires counties and cities within metropolitan areas to levy local income taxes on a cooperative
basis similar to that recommended by the ACIR. New York
City and Baltimore have the highest marginal tax rates,

TABLE III

MAXIMUM MARGINAL RATES UNDER EXISTING STATE INCOME TAXES
DECEMBER 31, 1968

State	Net income after personal exemption	Rate	State	Net income after personal exemption	Rate
Alabama	Over $ 5,000	5.0%	Minnesota	Over $ 20,000	12.0%
Alaska	16% of fed. income tax		Mississippi	" 5,000	4.0
Arizona	Over 6,000	8.0	Missouri	" 9,000	4.0
Arkansas	" 25,000	5.0	Montana	" 25,000	10.0
California	" 14,000	10.0	Nebraska	10% of fed. income tax	
Colorado	" 10,000	8.0	New Hampshire	Int. + div.	4.25
Delaware	" 100,000	11.0	New Jersey	Over 23,000	14.0
Georgia	" 10,000	6.0	New Mexico	" 100,000	6.0
Hawaii	" 30,000	11.0	New York	" 23,000	14.0
Idaho	" 5,000	9.0	North Carolina	" 10,000	7.0
Indiana	AGI	2.0	North Dakota	" 15,000	11.0
Iowa	Over 9,000	5.25	Oklahoma	" 7,500	6.0
Kansas	" 7,000	6.5	Oregon	" 8,000	9.5
Kentucky	" 8,000	6.0	South Carolina	" 10,000	7.0
Louisiana	" 50,000	6.0	Tennessee	Int. + div.	6.0
Maryland	" 3,000	5.0	Utah	Over 5,000	6.5
	Earned income	4.0	Vermont	25% of fed. income tax	
Massachusetts	Earnings on		Virginia	Over 5,000	5.0
	intangibles	8.0	West Virginia	" 200,000	5.5
Michigan	All taxable inc.	2.6	Wisconsin	" 14,000	10.0

States without a state income tax: Connecticut, Florida, Illinois, Maine, Nevada, Ohio, Pennsylvania, Rhode Island, South Dakota, Texas, Washington and Wyoming.

Source: ACIR, op. cit., note to Table II. See Table 35, pp. 78-84, *State and Local Finances...*

both enacted in 1966. In both cities, there has been
concern about the taxes' impact on the relocation of
high-income residents. The following comments by a
group of New York City residents exemplify this concern:

> The proposal to enact a personal income
> tax based on the present state law, but
> at one-half the rates, to be applied to
> both residents and commuters, is in our
> opinion unreasonable in the burden it
> places on individuals in the middle and
> upper income brackets--the very same
> groups that have tended to leave New
> York City in the past. While commuters
> may be asked to make a greater contribu-
> tion to the support of the City where
> they earn their living, a highly progres-
> sive tax of this nature is certain to act
> as an incentive to work outside New York
> City, or to demand pay adequate to cover
> its cost.[10]

Other major cities in New York, Pennsylvania, Ohio,
Kentucky, Missouri and Michigan have imposed local income
taxes without the simultaneous enactment of identical
taxes in the surrounding metropolitan area. This disparity has probably resulted in some emigration by city
dwellers seeking to escape the local income tax, but the
movement has not yet been significant enough to lead to
the repeal of local income taxes in the central cities.
Three factors have helped to minimize such emigration.
First, low rates have limited the incentive to relocate.
Second, most local income taxes apply to the income
earned in the city, regardless of the worker's residence.
Third, particularly in Pennsylvania, suburbs surrounding
the central city often follow its lead, quickly imposing
comparable local income taxes. Hence the incentive to
flee the city for the suburbs has been somewhat reduced.

The ACIR Recommendations: A Summary

The applicability of the ACIR recommendations for metropolitan coordination of local income taxes is limited by three factors. First, the recommendations can be implemented only in those states imposing state income taxes, but several states with large metropolitan areas, e.g., Washington, Illinois, Texas, Ohio and Pennsylvania, have no personal income taxes. Second, the recommendations would tie local revenues to the state income tax base. As changes in the state income tax law have direct bearing upon local revenues, the local jurisdictions would lose some of their independence. Finally, in those states with relatively progressive income taxes, a local supplement large enough to raise significant revenues might stimulate major relocation of both businesses and households.

However, adoption of the ACIR recommendations might be beneficial to some metropolitan areas. In some states, a local supplement of less than 50 percent could raise significant revenues, yet have little effect on location decisions. In other cases, where state income taxes are less progressive, a 50 percent supplement could be enacted without generating major relocation.

MAIN FEATURES OF EXISTING LOCAL INCOME TAX LAWS

Currently, there are four distinct types of local taxes on personal and business income: (1) a flat-rate tax on income earned within the local jurisdiction; (2) a flat-rate tax on both earned and unearned income; (3) a graduated tax on earned and unearned income, with a tax base differing in some particulars from that used by the state and (4) a local tax levied as a supplement to a state income tax.[11]

Local Flat-Rate Taxes on Earned Income

This is the form most commonly used in the United States, and appears in Pennsylvania, Ohio, Missouri,

Kentucky and Alabama. The majority of flat-rate taxes
are levied at 1.0 percent, but levels range from .25
to 2.0 percent.[12]

The definition of "earned income" varies little from
state to state. Salaries, wages, commissions and other
compensation received during the tax period are subject
to the tax, as are all net profits of unincorporated
businesses and professions. Deductions and exemptions
for dependents are rarely allowed.[13] However, specific
types of income may be exempted from the tax. These
have generally included pay or allowances to active members of the armed forces of the United States, relief
payments, unemployment insurance benefits, old age pensions, disability benefits, proceeds from insurance policies, earnings of minors and income of religious,
charitable and other nonprofit organizations.

In some cases, including Pennsylvania (but with the
exception of Philadelphia), the jurisdiction of one's
domicile has the exclusive right to tax his earnings. In
other cases, including Ohio, the legal provisions are
unclear, but credits have been evolved to prevent double
taxation of the individual who lives and works in different jurisdictions. In neither Kentucky nor Alabama do
local governments have the right to tax individuals'
incomes earned outside their jurisdiction. The taxes
are levied as occupational license taxes; hence, the
right to do business or be employed is being taxed, not
the income earned.

To the core city it may be important whether the
place of domicile or the place of work holds priority in
the taxation of earnings. In Pennsylvania, where the
jurisdiction of domicile holds priority and where the
total local income tax rate cannot exceed one percent
(Philadelphia is an exception on both counts), revenues
from the core city local income tax may be gradually
eroded as the surrounding suburbs enact their own one
percent income taxes.

Local governments in the five states also tax
business income at a flat rate. In Ohio, Missouri and

Kentucky, the business tax applies to corporate income
as well as to income from unincorporated businesses and
professions. In Pennsylvania, however, a prohibition in
the enabling act prevents local taxation of corporate
income, while the Gadsden, Alabama, ordinance does not
include corporate taxation.

Where flat-rate taxes on corporate income do exist,
they are generally levied at a rate identical to that on
personal earnings. In fact, in *Youngstown Sheet and Tube
Company v. City of Youngstown, Ohio*, the Ohio Appeals
Court ruled that in the absence of a reasonable basis for
discrimination, the rate must be the same as that levied
on individual income or net profits of unincorporated
businesses.[14]

Determining what portion of corporate earnings has
been generated within the municipality is always difficult. In some cases, business records provide a reasonable approximation of the income arising within a given
area. But since many corporations lack such bookkeeping
methods, formulae had to be developed to apportion net
profits to various jurisdictions. The "Massachusetts
Formula" is most commonly used. It allocates income by
calculating the percentage of the corporate total real
and personal property (the value of rented and leased
property is generally included), that may be allocated
to the city, then the percent of total gross receipts and
total payrolls. These figures are averaged to produce
the percent of corporate net profits taxable by the city.

Local Flat-Rate Taxes on Earned and Unearned Income

In 1964 the Michigan Legislature enacted a Uniform
Local Income Tax Ordinance that ensures uniformity among
all local income taxes imposed in the state. In those
cities in the state where a local income tax has been
enacted, both earned and unearned income of residents is
taxed at one percent. Income earned within the city by
nonresidents is taxed at 0.5 percent.[15] These taxes
differ in three fundamental ways from those levied in

Ohio and Pennsylvania. First, unearned income from
dividends, interest, net capital gains, income from
estates and trusts, and net profits from rentals of real
and tangible personal property are all taxable. Second,
the individual taxpayer is allowed deductions for the
full personal and dependency exemptions authorized by the
federal internal revenue code. Third, expenses neces-
sarily incurred in earning income may be deducted from
gross income in determining taxable income.

The tax credit permitted in the Uniform Local Income
Tax Ordinance ensures that no individual will be subject
to a total local tax rate in excess of one percent. The
individual subject to two local income taxes, one where
he lives, the other where he works, pays 0.5 percent to
the jurisdiction of employment, 0.5 percent to the
jurisdiction of domicile.

Cities in Michigan tax both corporate and noncorporate income at a one percent rate. The income of
unincorporated businesses is taxed not as business
income, but as personal income earned by the proprietor
or partner. In both cases, the Massachusetts Formula
is applied to apportion earnings among jurisdictions.
In Michigan, as in other states, the formula is used only
if the company's bookkeeping methods do not make readily
clear what part of net profits came from business conducted within the city.

Graduated Local Taxes on
Earned and Unearned Income

The City of New York imposes a graduated tax on the
earned and unearned income of residents. Subject to
several modifications, the New York City ordinance
defines a resident's city adjusted gross income (AGI) as
his federal AGI according to federal law for the tax
year.[16] The modifications which, for a given taxpayer,
may result in a local AGI that is either higher or lower
than federal AGI, are so numerous that they cannot all
be listed here. Among the more important modifications

permitted by the ordinance are the addition of interest
earned on state and local securities to the federal AGI;
and the deduction of both pensions to state employees
and interest on United States securities. Itemized
deductions similar to those on federal tax returns may
be used: The standard deduction is $1000 or 10 percent
of City AGI, whichever is smaller. An exemption of $600
is allowed for each dependent claimed on the federal
return.

New York City income tax rates are slightly progressive. They rise from 0.4 percent on the first $1000 of
taxable income to 2.0 percent on taxable income over
$30,000. Rates levied on commuters tend to be less
progressive. Most commuters are subject to a 0.25 percent rate levied on their salaries and wages, while self-
employed are subject to a 0.375 percent rate. Exemptions
for commuters are calculated on a sliding scale: $3000
on incomes under $10,000; $2000 on those between $10,000
and $20,000; $1000 on those between $20,000 and $30,000;
and none on those above $30,000.[17] No credits are
allowed for income taxes paid to other local jurisdictions.

Net profits of unincorporated businesses in New York
City are taxed as personal income. The tax on corporate
profits is a flat 5.5 percent, a rate higher than the
highest marginal rate on personal income. Methods for
determining what share of business income should be allocated to the city are similar to those discussed above.

Local Income Taxes Levied as
Supplements to a State Income Tax

Baltimore, Maryland, is the only American city
levying an income tax as a supplement to a state income
tax. It is the only city for which the state administers
and collects the tax, although the Michigan Legislature
enacted a law that would permit the state to collect
municipal income taxes starting in 1970. The Baltimore
tax is a 50 percent surtax on the Maryland state income

tax. Both earned and unearned income of residents is taxed, while nonresidents go untaxed. Rates range from one percent on the first $1000 of taxable income to 2.5 percent on taxable income over $3000. Deductions of $800 are permitted for each exemption claimed on the federal return, and an exemption is allowed for students regardless of age or income. A standard deduction of $1000 or 10 percent of AGI, whichever is less, is permitted. The income of unincorporated businesses is taxed as personal income, while taxation of corporate income in Maryland is reserved to the state.[18]

Due to its low administrative and compliance costs, the Baltimore tax has been carefully studied by other local governments. Several counties in Maryland levy similar taxes, with the surtax rate ranging from 20 to 50 percent of the state tax. Following the example of Maryland, New Mexico in 1968 authorized counties to levy a county income surtax of up to 50 percent of the state income tax, with voter approval. Two basic similarities exist between the Baltimore income tax and that recommended by the ACIR: The tax is administered by a state tax collecting agency, and the local tax is levied as a percent of the state tax.

NOTES TO CHAPTER I

1. Major cities are those with populations in excess of 100,000 in 1960. Sources: Tax Foundation, Inc., *City Income Taxes* (New York: 1967); U.S. Advisory Commission on Intergovernmental Relations, *State and Local Finances, Significant Features, 1966 to 1969* (Washington, D.C.: 1968).

2. Ohio Municipal League, *Statistics on Municipal Income Taxes in Ohio* (Columbus: 1967), pp. 11-15.

3. See U.S. Advisory Commission on Intergovernmental Relations, note 1 above, p. 95.

4. See Ohio Municipal League, note 2 above, p. 13.

5. Ohio Municipal League, *Staff Report Number 3, Statistical Data--Property and Income Taxes, Rates, Collections and Valuations* (Columbus: n.d.), Table III Income Tax Data, n.p.

6. Ohio Municipal League, *First Revised Model Income Tax Ordinance* (Columbus: 1959).

7. Michigan, State Legislature, *Public and Local Acts*, Regular Session of 1964, "Act Number 284," pp. 537-556.

8. New York, *Laws of New York, Chapter 773*, 1966.

9. U.S. Advisory Commission on Intergovernmental Relations, *State and Local Taxes, Significant Features, 1968* (Washington, D.C.: 1968), p. 211.

10. Economic Development Council of New York City, Inc., *An Analysis of the Impact of Taxes on Jobs in New York City*, Policy Study Number 1 (New York: 1966), p. 11.

11.   Appendix Table A summarizes major provisions of city income tax regulations for cities with population over 100,000.

12.   Appendix Table B indicates tax rates for local governments in nine states.

13.   Springfield, Ohio treats earned income up to $1040 as tax-free, but taxes the entire sum if income exceeds $1040.

14.   Ohio Court of Appeals, Seventh District, *Youngstown Sheet and Tube Company v. City of Youngstown* (November 1951).   See Robert A. Sigafoos, *The Municipal Income Tax: Its History and Problems* (Chicago: Public Administration Service, 1955), p. 97.

15.   The Detroit rate has been increased to 2 percent for the period October 1, 1968 to December 31, 1970.

16.   New York, *Laws of New York, Chapter 773*, Article 2-D, Part II, Section 12, p. 2113.

17.   Edwin G. Michaelian, "Comments," *The Municipal Income Tax, Proceedings of the Academy of Political Science*, 28(4): 478-480 (1968), especially p. 478.

18.   Letter from Richard E. Maine for Charles L. Benton, Director of Finance, Baltimore, Maryland, March 4, 1969. From July 1, 1966 to June 30, 1967, Baltimore did levy a one percent tax on net profits earned in Baltimore by both incorporated and unincorporated businesses.

Appendix to Chapter I

TABLE A

LOCAL INCOME TAXES, RATES AND COLLECTIONS
(Dollar amounts in thousands)

State and local government*	Rate December 31, 1968 (percent)	Municipal tax collections, 1966-67 (Cities with over 50,000 population in 1960)		
		Total tax collections	Income tax collections Amount	As a percent of total collections
Alabama				
Gadsden	2.0	$ 4,040	$ 2,296	56.8
Kentucky				
Berea	1.5	a	a	a
Bowling Green	1.0	a	a	a
Catlettsburg	1.0	a	a	a
Covington	1.75	2,827	851	30.1
Flemingsburg	0.5	a	a	a
Frankfort	1.0	a	a	a
Fulton	1.0	a	a	a
Glasgow	1.0	a	a	a
Hopkinsville	1.0	a	a	a
Lexington	1.5	7,965	4,215	52.9
Louisville	1.25	29,182	15,072	51.6
Jefferson County[b]	1.75	a	a	a
Ludlow	1.0	a	a	a
Mayfield	0.67	a	a	a
Maysville	1.0	a	a	a
Middlesboro	1.0	a	a	a
Newport	2.0	a	a	a
Owensboro	1.0	a	a	a
Paducah	1.25	a	a	a

	% of state tax			
Pikeville	1.0	a	a	a
Princeton	1.0	a	a	a
Richmond	1.0	a	a	a
Maryland				
Baltimore City	50	177,904	24,804	13.9
2 counties	20	a	a	a
1 county	25	a	a	a
1 county	30	a	a	a
5 counties	35	a	a	a
1 county	40	a	a	a
5 counties	45	a	a	a
8 counties	50	a	a	a
Michigan				
Battle Creek	c	a	a	a
Detroit	c,d	154,295	46,482	30.1
Flint	c	16,171	8,513	52.6
Grand Rapids	c	9,082	e	e
Hamtramck	c	a	a	a
Highland Park	c	7,594	e	e
Lansing	c	a	a	a
Lapeer	c	5,766	e	e
Pontiac	c	a	a	a
Port Huron[f]	c	a	a	a
Saginaw	c	6,447	3,107	48.2
Missouri				
Kansas City	0.5	43,894	10,646	24.3
St. Louis	1.0	84,304	28,754	34.1
New Mexico[g]				

TABLE A (cont.)

LOCAL INCOME TAXES, RATES AND COLLECTIONS
(Dollar amounts in thousands)

State and local government*	Rate December 31, 1968 (percent)	Total tax collections	Municipal tax collections, 1966-67 (Cities with over 50,000 population in 1960)	
			Amount	As a percent of total collections
New York				
New York City	0.4 - 2.0^h	$2,443,891	$329,327	13.5
Ohio				
Akron	1.0	19,450	10,777	55.4
Canton	1.3^i	5,772	4,335	75.1
Cincinnati	1.0	46,992	18,962	40.4
Cleveland	1.0	59,998	e	e
Cleveland Heights	1.0	3,377	e	e
Columbus	1.0	24,163	17,481	72.3
Dayton	1.0	24,615	14,387	58.4
Euclid	0.5	3,829	e	e
Hamilton	1.0	3,192	1,822	57.1
Kettering	1.0	1,949	e	e
Lakewood	1.0	3,092	e	e
Lima	1.0	1,888	1,241	65.7
Lorain	0.5	2,556	e	e
Parma	1.0	3,295	e	e
Springfield	1.0	3,989	2,784	69.8
Toledo	1.5	20,496	11,774	57.4
Warren	1.0	3,060	2,158	70.5
Youngstown	1.5	9,047	4,901	54.2

		a	a	a
184 cities and villages (with less than 50,000 population)	0.25 - 1.5	a	a	a
Pennsylvania[j]				
Abington Township	1.0[k]	2,289	e	e
Allentown	1.0[k]	5,851	1,629	27.8
Altoona	1.0[l]	2,663	519	19.5
Bethlehem	1.0[l]	3,891	664	17.1
Chester	1.0[m]	2,987	1,297	43.4
Erie	1.0[k]	8,033	1,712	21.3
Harrisburg	1.0[k]	4,315	757	17.5
Johnstown	1.0[l]	2,191	418	19.1
Lancaster	0.5[n]	2,196	567	25.8
Penn Hill Township	1.0[l]	1,769	652	36.9
Philadelphia	2.0[m]	254,998	118,770	46.6
Pittsburgh	1.0[k]	52,736	10,946	20.8
Scranton	1.0[k,o]	4,838	914	18.9
Wilkes Barre	1.0[k]	2,489	81	3.3
York	1.0[k]	2,176	474	21.8
Approx. 3100 other local jurisdictions (including over 1000 school districts)	0.25 - 1.0	a	a	a

*Note: Excludes Washington, D.C. which has a graduated net income tax more closely akin to a state tax than to the municipal income taxes.

[a] Signifies a county, or cities under 50,000 population.

[b] A taxpayer subject to the 1.25 percent tax imposed by the City of Louisville may credit this tax against the 1.75 percent levied by Jefferson County.

[c] Under the Michigan "Uniform City Income Tax Act," the prescribed rates are 1.0 percent for residents and 0.5 percent for nonresidents. A resident is allowed credit for taxes paid to another city as a nonresident.

[d] The rate for residents in Detroit was increased from 1 percent to 2 percent from October 1, 1968 to December 31, 1970.

TABLE A (cont.)

^{e}Tax went into effect after reporting period.

^{f}New tax effective January 1, 1969.

^{g}The 1968 Legislature empowered local school boards to impose a county income surtax up to the maximum of 50 percent of the state income tax, subject to approval by the electorate. The surtax, if imposed, will be state collected and will not apply to corporations. Authorization is limited to the calendar year 1968 or any fiscal year commencing in 1968. No school board had imposed such a tax by mid-November of 1968.

^{h}New York City residents' rate ranges from 0.4 percent on taxable income of less than $1000 to 2.0 percent on taxable income in excess of $30,000. An earnings tax of 0.25 percent of wages or 3/8 of one percent on net earnings from self-employment, not to exceed that which would be due if taxpayer were a resident, is levied against nonresidents.

^{i}The Canton rate is 1.3 percent from September 1, 1968 through December 31, 1968; 1.4 percent for 1969; and 1.5 percent thereafter.

^{j}Except for Philadelphia, Pittsburgh and Scranton, the total rate payable by any taxpayer is limited to one percent. For coterminous jurisdictions, such as borough and borough school district, the maximum is usually divided equally between the jurisdictions unless otherwise agreed. However, school districts may tax only residents. Thus, if a borough and a coterminous school district each have a stated rate of one percent, the total effective rate for residents is one percent (1/2 of one percent each to the borough and school district) and the tax on nonresidents is one percent, the stated rate imposed by the borough.

^{k}The school district rate is the same as the municipal rate.

^{l}The school district rate is 0.5 percent.

^{m}There is no school district income tax.

^{n}The school district rate is 1.0 percent.

^{o}Combined city and school district rate may not exceed 2.0 percent.

Source: U.S. Advisory Commission on Intergovernmental Relations, *State and Local Finances, Significant Features, 1966 to 1969* (Washington, D.C.: November 1968), pp. 95-97.

TABLE B

MAJOR PROVISIONS OF CITY INCOME TAX REGULATIONS: CITIES WITH POPULATION IN EXCESS OF 100,000--1967

| City | Nonresident rate relative to resident rate | Business taxed[a] | | Resident income base includes: | | | | Reciprocal city tax credit allowed | Personal exemptions allowed | Personal deductions allowed | Tax withheld on wages and salaries |
		Incorporated	Unincorporated	Wages, salaries, similar income only	Income earned out of jurisdiction	Capital gains	Dividends				
New York, N.Y.	b	Yes	Yes	No	Yes	Yes	Yes	No	$600 ea.[b]	Yes	Yes
Philadelphia, Pa.	Same	No	Yes	Yes	Yes	No	No	No	No	No	Yes
Detroit, Mich.	Half	Yes	Yes	No	Yes	Yes	Yes	Yes	$600 ea.	No	Yes
Baltimore, Md.	Zero	Yes	Yes	No	Yes	Yes	Yes	No	$800 ea.	Yes	Yes
Cleveland, Ohio	Same	Yes	Yes	Yes	Yes	No	No	Yes	No	No	Yes
St. Louis, Mo.	Same	Yes	Yes	Yes	Yes	No	No[c]	No	No	No	Yes
Cincinnati, Ohio	Same	No	Yes	No	Yes	No	No	Yes	No	No	Yes
Pittsburgh, Pa.	Same	Yes	Yes	Yes	No	No	No[c]	Yes	No	No	Yes
Kansas City, Mo.	Same	Yes	Yes	No	Yes	No	No	Yes	No	No	Yes
Columbus, Ohio	Same	Yes	Yes	Yes	Yes	No	No	Yes	No	No	Yes
Louisville, Ky.	Same	Yes	Yes	No	No	No[c]	No	No	No	No	Yes
Toledo, Ohio	Same	Yes	Yes	Yes	Yes	No	No	Yes	No	No	Yes
Akron, Ohio	Same	Yes	Yes	Yes	Yes	No	No	No	No	No	Yes
Dayton, Ohio	Same	Yes	Yes	Yes	Yes	No	No	Yes	No	No	Yes
Flint, Mich.	Half	Yes	Yes	No	Yes	Yes	Yes	Yes	$600 ea.	No	Yes
Youngstown, Ohio	Same	Yes	Yes	Yes	Yes	No	No	Yes	No	No	Yes
Erie, Pa.	Same	No	Yes	No	Yes	No	No	Yes	No	No	Yes
Canton, Ohio	Same	Yes	Yes	Yes	Yes	No	No	Yes	No	No	Yes
Scranton, Pa.	Same	No	Yes	Yes	Yes	No	No	No	No	No	Yes
Allentown, Pa.	Same	No	Yes	Yes	Yes	No	No	Yes	No	No	Yes
Grand Rapids, Mich.	Half	Yes	Yes	No	Yes	Yes	Yes	Yes	$600 ea.	No	Yes

[a] Charitable, religious, educational, and other nonprofit organizations exempt in most cases. Tax generally confined to income stemming from activities in city.

[b] Nonresidents taxed on different basis from residents. The rate is markedly lower, instead of deductions, an exclusion related to income level is allowed. The exclusion of $3000 on income up to $10,000 drops to $2000 for income over $10,000, to $1000 for $20,000-$30,000 income, to none for income over $30,000.

[c] Except where derived in connection with the conduct of a business.

Source: Tax Foundation, Inc., City Income Taxes (New York: 1967), p. 23. Table compiled by the foundation from Commerce Clearing House data and information obtained directly from city officials.

 **II**

Local Income Taxes: Some Aspects Considered

ADMINISTRATIVE COSTS

The administrative costs of local income taxes vary greatly, depending on the complexity and unfamiliarity of the tax and the scale and efficiency of the collecting agency. For 330 local tax jurisdictions in Pennsylvania, John W. Cook found that average collection costs ranged from 6.0 percent of revenues collected in jurisdictions collecting less than $50,000, to 3.9 percent in jurisdictions collecting more than $200,000.[1] As Table IV indicates, the variation in collection costs was wide, even in jurisdictions collecting comparable revenues. Cook suggests that the highest figures probably represent districts levying the tax for the first time, while the low figures frequently reflect incomplete reporting of costs. John Gotherman of the Ohio Municipal League estimates the costs as generally lower in Ohio.[2] He estimates that at a tax rate of one percent the administrative costs are about 2 percent of collections. At a one-half percent rate, they would be approximately 4 percent.

Size of the Tax Base

The size of the local tax base is one of the most important factors limiting administrative costs. In Detroit the large tax base helps keep administrative costs low despite a relatively complicated form of taxation. A.L. Warren, Director of the Income Tax Division of the City of Detroit, reported that the direct costs

TABLE IV

COSTS OF COLLECTING LOCAL INCOME TAXES
AS A PERCENTAGE OF THE TAX COLLECTIONS
FOR PENNSYLVANIA JURISDICTIONS

Costs of collection as a percent of total	Total collections				
	More than $200,000	$100,000 to $200,000	$50,000 to $100,000	Less than $50,000	All
Average	3.9	5.0	5.9	6.0	4.4
Low	0.8	1.8	0.7	0.5	0.5
High	8.6	10.5	24.8	20.2	24.8

Source: See note 1, this chapter.

of administering the tax in 1966 amounted to 2.2 percent of net revenues, the total costs being 3.2 percent.[3] Because of very large revenues New York City was able to cut administrative costs to less than one percent of collections by not requiring returns to be filed by commuters or those residents who earned less than $8000 in wages and had not more than $300 in other income.[4] The incomes of these individuals are, however, still subject to withholding.

Collection Agency

Administrative costs are also affected by the agency collecting the tax. In several states--Michigan, Ohio and Pennsylvania--cities collect their own income taxes, largely because state income taxes had not been adopted at the time the local ones were enacted.[5] New York City also collects its own income tax, despite the existence of a state tax collection agency. Ira H. Jolles, Director of the New York City Income Tax Bureau, believes that transfer of collection responsibilities to the state would save the city from $3 to $5 million, even if the city covers the state's additional costs.[6]

Withholding

Another factor that lowers administrative costs is the tax withholding performed by business. Among the Ohio communities levying local income taxes, the percentage of income tax revenues withheld in 1966 ranged from 35 percent in Elmore to 100 percent in Fairfax and Holland. For the four major cities of Cincinnati, Columbus, Toledo and Dayton, the shares of total income tax collections withheld ranged from 74.2 to 80.0 percent.[7] In such cases a large percentage of local income tax revenue is collected at the expense of local businesses.

Simplicity

A final factor that limits administrative costs is the simplicity of the tax. Local income taxes in Ohio, Pennsylvania, Kentucky, Missouri and Alabama are usually levied at flat rates and apply only to earned income. There is no provision for either deductions or exemptions. Administrative costs are also minimized by Maryland's local income taxes which are surtaxes on the state income tax, and are collected by the state itself. The New York City tax, on the other hand, includes provisions for deductions, exemptions, taxation of unearned income, graduated tax rates and a differential tax on commuters. While perhaps increasing the equity of the tax, these refinements have measurably increased the costs of administration.

But even under the most unfavorable conditions--local collection of a complicated tax--administrative costs are not high enough to prohibit the use of local income taxes. Evidence indicates that a large city that taxes earned and unearned income and allows exemptions can prevent administrative costs from rising much above 2 or 3 percent of total collections. In comparison, "good" property tax administration in the larger jurisdictions should be possible with costs rising very little above 1.5 percent of revenues.[8] Administrative costs of state retail sales taxes have generally been below 2

percent: In 1960, only New Mexico had a higher administrative cost.[9] As would be expected, the administrative
costs were highest in those states with the lowest tax
rates. Thus the administrative costs of local income
taxes are slightly higher than those for well-
administered property taxes or state-administered
sales taxes, but this cost may be more than offset by
the equity and revenue-raising ability of the local
income tax.

COMPLIANCE COSTS

Each individual and each business--where taxes are
levied on business income--must take the time and effort
required to complete the necessary forms. One official
closely involved with the tax collections states that
"the municipal income tax, because of its low rates, is
more of a psychological irritant than a pecuniary one."[10]
But for those whose "time is money," or those who pay to
have their forms completed, the local income tax imposes
financial burdens beyond those of the tax itself.[11]

Businesses operating in a number of taxing jurisdictions face the special problem of dividing their taxable
income among taxing jurisdictions. The burden of the
additional bookkeeping and reporting required is often
greater than that of the tax payment, with the result
that many businesses simply fail to comply.[12] A congres-
sional Special Subcommittee on State Taxation of Interstate Commerce found that almost all corporations filed
local income tax returns in only one tax jurisdiction--
the location of the actual physical plant.[13] Most local
ordinances, including those in Michigan and Ohio, impose
a liability on all corporations doing business in the
city, whether or not they have a physical plant there.
Nevertheless, only the largest corporations comply fully
with these ordinances. For many smaller businesses the
cost of compliance is apparently greater than the risk
of prosecution.

A recent study of state and local taxes in Montana
illustrates the burden of compliance costs.[14] Table V,

TABLE V
ADMINISTRATIVE AND COMPLIANCE
COSTS FOR VARIOUS MONTANA TAXES

Type of tax	Compliance cost as percent of revenue	Administrative cost as percent of revenue	Total cost
	(percent)	(percent)	(percent)
Personal income tax	29.0	2.1	31.1
Corporate income tax	10.2	0.4	10.6
Property tax (except motor vehicle)	2.8	6.7	9.5
Motor vehicle tax	7.7	6.7	14.4
Cigarette tax	2.7	0.04	2.7
Sales tax[a]	2.5	2.0	4.5

[a]Montana lacks a general sales and use tax. Its sales tax estimates are taken from J.A. Maxwell's *Financing State and Local Government* (Washington, D.C.: Brookings, 1965), p. 95.

Source: See note 14, this chapter.

based on the Montana data, indicates that compliance costs are higher for income taxes than for any other form of tax. While the costs may not be particularly onerous to businesses whose bookkeeping procedures are already mechanized to deal with withholding, individuals and smaller businesses may find the compliance costs unreasonable.

The actual extent of compliance costs, like that of administrative costs, will depend on the size, complexity and unfamiliarity of the tax imposed. Complicated tax forms, providing for deductions, exemptions and graduated rates, increase compliance costs, as does the imposition of even the simplest new tax. In addition, the same amount of bookkeeping labor is required whatever the tax rate. Hence compliance costs as a percent of revenues raised will decline as the tax rate increases.

EFFECTS ON LOCATION DECISIONS
OF BUSINESSES AND HOUSEHOLDS

In the 1950s and early 1960s students of local income taxes agreed that such taxes appeared to have no noticeable effect on the location decisions of businesses and households.[15] In the last decade, however, taxes have been applied to unearned income, and tax rates have risen significantly. As late as 1961 the highest rate levied on earned income was Philadelphia's 1 5/8 percent. But since that time there has been a slow but steady upward trend in local income tax rates.

Table VI indicates that in 17 out of 24 cases the local income tax rate rose between 1954 and 1969. In no case did the tax rate fall. These changes suggest the need for a reexamination of the behavior of the commercial, industrial and residential sectors in those cities that use local income taxes.

Dayton, Ohio, provides one case of rising opposition to increased local income tax rates. As the local tax rate increased in Dayton, it was opposed by increasingly larger percentages of the population. In 1950, 75.07 percent of the voters approved an ordinance providing a .05 percent income tax; 76.55 percent voted to renew the rate in a special election in 1954.[16] However, as Table VII shows, by 1959 an ordinance raising the rate to .75 percent was approved by only 55.71 percent of the voters; in 1964 an increase to one percent was approved by only 51.59 percent.

Dayton, however, did not reduce or repeal its local income tax. Despite rising local income tax rates, the writer's correspondence substantiates earlier views on relocation effects. Chamber of Commerce officials unanimously agreed that local income taxes had not slowed the expansion of business activities in their communities. Lower property tax rates and additional public services were frequently cited as offsetting the negative effect of the local income tax.

TABLE VI

A COMPARISON OF 1954 WITH 1969 LOCAL INCOME
TAX RATES FOR SELECTED CITIES:
1960 POPULATIONS IN EXCESS OF 25,000

City	1954 Tax rate	1969 Tax rate	Percent increase in tax rate, 1954 to 1969
St. Louis, Mo.	0.5	1.0	100
Cincinnati, O.	1.0	1.0	0
Pittsburgh, Pa.	1.0	1.0	0
Philadelphia, Pa.	1.25	2.0	60
Louisville, Ky.	1.0	1.25	25
Columbus, O.	0.5	1.0	100
Canton, O.	0.6	1.4	133
Dayton, O.	0.5	1.0	100
Toledo, O.	1.0	1.5	50
Youngstown, O.	0.5	1.5	200
Erie, Pa.	0.5	1.0	100
Scranton, Pa.	0.5	0.5	0
Lexington, Ky.	1.5	1.5	0
Altoona, Pa.	0.5	1.0	100
Johnstown, Pa.	0.5	1.0	100
Springfield, O.	0.6	1.0	67
Warren, O.	0.5	1.0	100
Newport, Ky.	1.0	2.0	100
Paducah, Ky.	0.5	1.25	150
Barberton, O.	0.5	1.0	100
Norwood, Ky.	1.0	1.0	0
New Castle, Pa.	1.0	1.0	0
Sharon, Pa.	1.0	1.0	0
Williamsport, Pa.	0.125	0.5	300

Source: See Sigafoos, Ch. I note 14 above, pp. 72-73; and note to Table II above, p. 95.

TABLE VII

VOTING RECORD ON EARNED INCOME TAX
ORDINANCES IN DAYTON, OHIO

Date	Tax rate	Votes against	Percent	Votes for	Percent
7-1-50	1/2%	11,036	24.93	33,242	75.07
5-4-54	1/2% (renewed)	5,351	23.45	17,463	76.55
3-24-59	3/4% (1/4% rise)	17,545	44.79	22,069	55.21
5-5-64	1% (1/4% rise)	19,149	48.41	20,401	51.59

Source: See note 16, this chapter.

From Lexington, Kentucky, a city that has levied an income tax at a 1.5 percent rate since 1952, came this report:

> Not one single business has left town because of it...and indeed, our first major industrial prospect was landed in 1956, that being IBM. Following IBM in quick succession...[were] Square D Company, Trane, Dixie Cup, Westinghouse, Vogue Rattan, Semicon Associates, accompanied with a phenomenal growth rate.... I think a run-down city with poor public services (police, fire, streets, etc.) would have a more detrimental effect in terms of business climate than does a 1½ per cent tax properly utilized to maintain the community.[17]

From Louisville, Kentucky:

> We have no...[documentary] evidence
> that the local income taxes have ever
> influenced businesses to locate beyond
> the local income tax area. In fact,
> the manager of our Industrial Develop-
> ment Department knows of no instance
> when the local income tax has been
> questioned as a deterrent.... In view
> of the rather light local tax burden
> on property the application of the
> income tax on business net profits has
> not been particularly objectionable.[18]

From Cincinnati, Ohio:

> We cannot point to any specific instance
> where the existence of a local income
> tax has been a factor in the location
> of a payroll in our area. We do not
> doubt that it *is* a factor but we have
> no experience to prove it. Our feeling
> is that the overall picture and the ser-
> vices available for those taxes are the
> controlling factors.[19]

From Warren, Ohio:

> We have no evidence that the city
> income tax has had any effect on the
> location of businesses nor has there
> been any voicing of opposition by
> businesses to the tax.[20]

And from Gadsden, Alabama:

> Our occupational tax...has not in any
> manner affected the growth of our
> community. As a matter of fact, con-
> siderable progress has been made since
> the tax has been imposed (1956). It

is obvious that more community developments which are attractive to our citizens have been installed.[21]

Such assertions do not prove that local income taxes
have no effect upon the decision of businesses to locate
in an area. In fact, taxes may receive more attention
from businessmen than their size would warrant. Chambers
of Commerce can easily provide tax information to businesses interested in locating in their area; business
magazines can compare local tax disadvantages. The exact
tax structure within a community will of course affect
businesses differently. Those with little taxable property and high earnings will be most adversely affected
by increasing reliance on local income taxes. Those with
much property and small earnings will be hurt by emphasis
on property taxation. Similarly, new businesses with
low earnings may favor income taxation, while well-
established businesses with high earnings would oppose
it.

Due to the scarcity of data available and the large
number of other variables affecting location decisions,
it is at the present time impossible to provide any
empirical measurement of the locational effects resulting
from local income tax enactment.[22]

NOTES TO CHAPTER II

1. Pennsylvania, Department of Internal Affairs, Bureau of Municipal Affairs, *The Administration of the Earned Income Tax* by John W. Cook (Harrisburg: 1964), p. 77.

2. See Ohio Municipal League, Ch. I note 2, Foreword.

3. "Detroit's Experience," *The Municipal Income Tax, Proceedings of the Academy of Political Science*, 28(4): 452-454 (1968), especially p. 454.

4. Mabel Walker, "The Inevitability of City Income Taxes," *Tax Policy*, 34(4,5): 3-12 (1967), p. 6.

5. The Michigan State Legislature has passed a law that permits the state government to collect local income tax revenues beginning January 1, 1970.

6. "Administration of the Municipal Income Tax," *The Municipal Income Tax, Proceedings of the Academy of Political Science*, 28(4): 471-477 (1968), especially p. 477.

7. See Ohio Municipal League, Ch. I note 2, pp. 27-31.

8. Dick Netzer, *Economics of the Property Tax* (Washington, D.C.: Brookings, 1966), p. 176.

9. National Tax Association, "Report of Committee on Cost of Taxpayer Compliance and Administration," *Proceedings of the 55th Annual Conference* (1962), pp. 300-301.

10. See Ira H. Jolles, note 6 above, p. 472.

11. See H.G. Homuth, "The Taxpayer Angle on Local Income Tax Administration," in *Income Tax Administration: Symposium* (New York: Tax Institute, 1949), pp. 329-349.

12. See U.S. Congress, House Committee on the Judiciary, *Report of the Special Subcommittee on State Taxation of Interstate Commerce*, Chapter 14, "Local Corporate Income Taxes," vol. I, pp. 441-480 (Washington, D.C.: 1966).

Harry P. Bugeja, Manager of the Tax Department for R.L. Polk & Co., wrote the following in a letter to the author: "So far as multi-state businesses are concerned, local income taxation, generally premised on an apportionment of profits, often constitutes more of a burden from an administrative rather than a cash outlay standpoint. While the obligation for such taxes, especially in the case of service businesses, is as extensive as the number of cities imposing such taxes, the amount of tax payable to such jurisdictions is quite often in the pennies. At the same time, however, the same amount of administrative work is required to develop the necessary data on which to determine the tax whether the tax is equal to pennies or to millions of dollars." (May 10, 1968.)

13. *Report*, note 12 above, pp. 441-480.

14. John H. Wicks and Michael N. Killworth, "Administrative and Compliance Costs of State and Local Taxes," *National Tax Journal*, 20(3): 309-315 (1967).

15. See Robert A. Sigafoos, Ch. I note 14, p. 129; Sigafoos, "The Stake of Business in the Growing Municipal Income Tax Movement" in *State and Local Taxes on Business* (Princeton: Tax Institute of America, 1965), pp. 113-125, see especially p. 119; Frederick D. Stocker, *Nonproperty Taxes as Sources of Local Revenue*, Bulletin 903 (Ithaca: Cornell University Agriculture Experiment Station, 1953), p. 67; Milton C. Taylor, *Local Income Taxes as a Source of Revenue for Michigan Cities* (East Lansing: Michigan State University, 1961), p. 27.

16. City of Dayton, Ohio, *Income Tax Ordinance No. 21420*, 1964.

17. Letter from D. Roy Gillespie, Executive Vice President of Lexington Chamber of Commerce, Lexington, Kentucky, April 19, 1968.

18. Letter from Richard K. Harb, Manager, Research Department, Louisville Chamber of Commerce, Louisville, Kentucky, April 15, 1968.

19. Letter from Kenneth M. Burch, Director, Economic Development, Greater Cincinnati Chamber of Commerce, Cincinnati, Ohio, April 23, 1968.

20. Letter from Frances E. Davis, Deputy Treasurer, City of Warren, Ohio, April 23, 1968.

21. Letter from Harold R. Laubscher, Manager, Gadsden Chamber of Commerce, Gadsden, Alabama, April 19, 1968.

22. Several attempts have been made to measure the locational effects of taxes. See Eva Mueller, A. Wilken, and M. Wood, *Location Decisions and Industrial Mobility in Michigan, 1961* (Ann Arbor: Institute of Social Research, University of Michigan, 1961); J.S. Floyd, *Effects of Taxation in Industrial Location* (Chapel Hill: University of North Carolina Press, 1952); Alan K. Campbell, "Taxes and Industrial Location in the New York Metropolitan Region," *National Tax Journal*, 11(3): 195-218 (1958); Paul W. McCracken, et al., *Taxes and Economic Growth in Michigan* (Kalamazoo: W.E. Upjohn Institute for Employment Research, 1960); John Due, "Studies of State-Local Tax Influences on Location of Industry," *National Tax Journal*, 14(2): 163-173 (1961).

Theoretical Effects on Resource
Allocation of a Local Income Tax

Studies of the vertical and horizontal equity of
local income taxes have relied for their methodology on
partial equilibrium analysis. Hence most attention was
focused on whether the tax increases or decreases the
real income of various classes of residents or nonresidents. In contrast, questions of resource allocation
that require the application of general equilibrium
analysis have been almost totally ignored. Yet little
can be said about the equity of a tax without examining
its impact on resource allocation. For example, how
would the replacement of a property tax by a local income
tax yielding an equal amount of revenue affect: (1) the
resource allocation resulting from the incidence of local
taxes on businesses; (2) incentives to work in the city;
(3) incentives to invest in the city; (4) the residential
location chosen by recipients of various classes of
income; (5) the value of real properties; and (6) relative price structures? These questions must be examined
before turning to the equity of local income taxes.*

---

* This chapter may be omitted by readers less interested
in the complex problems involved in predicting the
effects of a tax change. Although this chapter sheds
light on some of the limitations of empirical analysis,
it is not crucial to understanding the material that is
discussed later in the book.

THE EFFECT OF TAX CHANGES ON
THE DEMAND FOR BUSINESS PROPERTY

The Effect on Total Local Business Taxes

Even in those cases where the fear to try something
new initially created business opposition to local income
taxes, the business community has generally been satisfied with them once they have been imposed. The reason
can be seen in Table VIII. Consider a one percent tax on
the earned and unearned income of residents and the
earned income of nonresidents. If this were accompanied
by a 3 percent tax on the net income of all businesses
(a Type IX tax), businesses in San Francisco would pay
$21 million more in income taxes (column 4), but nearly
$29 million less in property taxes (column 3). The San
Francisco business community in general benefits from any
tax used to reduce property tax rates so long as other
sectors of the community pay approximately one-half of
the revenues.

A similar situation prevails in Detroit. Leonard D.
Bronder estimated that business would pay $11 million of
the $40 million to be raised by a local income tax.[1]
But if $40 million had been raised through property
taxes, business would have paid $24.5 million. By
accepting the local income tax as an alternative to
higher property tax rates, business paid $13.5 million
less in total taxes.

If business property accounts for a large portion
of the property tax base--and it usually does--business
will generally benefit from taxation of both personal and
business income at the local level. Table IX indicates
the business sector's share of the total assessed value
of real property in 42 large American cities. In 1966
this property accounted for one-third or more of total
locally assessed real property in 21 of the cities. And
in all but 8 of the 42 cities, the share of total
locally assessed real property belonging to business is
above 27.5 percent. When personalty is included in the
property tax base, the business share becomes still

TABLE VIII

THE EFFECT OF DIFFERENT TYPES OF LOCAL INCOME TAXES ON TOTAL
LOCAL BUSINESS TAXES IN SAN FRANCISCO IN 1967

(1) Type of local income tax[a]	(2) Local income tax revenues (thousands)	(3)=.52(2) Business property tax savings (thousands)	(4) Business income tax payment (thousands)	(5) Local tax savings for business[b] (thousands)
I	$34,870	$18,132	$ -	$18,132
II	29,820	15,506	-	15,506
III	28,370	14,752	-	14,752
IV	25,750	13,390	-	13,390
V	20,690	10,759	-	10,759
VI	39,476	20,528	4,606	15,922
VII	41,756	21,713	6,896	14,817
VIII	48,684	25,318	13,813	11,505
IX	55,586	28,905	20,638	8,217
X	23,000	11,960	-	11,960
XI	36,720	19,094	6,896	12,198

[a]For a description of income tax Types I through XI see Table XIII, p. 73.

[b]Before federal income tax offset.

Source: Table XIII.

TABLE IX

ASSESSED VALUE OF COMMERCIAL AND INDUSTRIAL REALTY AS
A PERCENT OF TOTAL LOCALLY ASSESSED REAL PROPERTY
IN THE 42 LARGEST CITIES IN THE U.S., 1966[a]

Newark	55.5	Denver	33.0
Boston	55.4	Seattle	33.0
Minneapolis	53.9	Portland	32.6
Cleveland	48.2	Louisville	32.4
Rochester	47.6	Cincinnati	31.9
St. Louis	47.6	Washington, D.C.	31.1
Pittsburgh	46.2	Indianapolis	31.1
Buffalo	44.7	Fort Worth	30.3[a]
San Francisco	43.5	Memphis	29.8
St. Paul	42.4	New Orleans	29.1
New York City	41.8	Houston	28.0[a]
Chicago	40.5	Los Angeles	26.8
Detroit	40.4	Norfolk	26.5
Atlanta	39.9	Columbus	26.2
Milwaukee	39.4	Omaha	26.2
Oakland	37.2	Toledo	24.1
Dallas	36.8[a]	San Diego	22.6
Kansas City	36.3	Oklahoma City	22.0
Birmingham	36.1	Long Beach	20.7
Philadelphia	35.3	San Antonio	18.5[a]
Baltimore	33.3	Phoenix	18.1

[a]Because 1966 data are not available for Texas cities,
1961 data are used.

Source: U.S. Bureau of the Census, Census of Governments, 1962 and 1967, *Taxable Property Values*, pp. 150-
152 (1962) and pp. 124-145 (1967).

higher. It seems likely that business property would account for less than 27.5 percent of total assessed property in only 5 of the 42 cases. Hence, it is likely that if income tax revenues were used to permit across-the-board reductions in property tax rates, the share of property tax reductions flowing to the business community would be larger than their share of income tax contributions.

At first glance, this lowering of total local taxes would appear to make business operations more profitable. But if the tax change affected the supply of labor adversely, or if it caused a major change in the demand for goods produced locally, it is quite possible that overall business conditions would be worsened. Thus market structure, wage pressure and changes in demand must all be examined to determine whether business would be likely to expand or contract in San Francisco as a result of the imposition of a local income tax.

The Role of Market Structure

Assuming temporarily that both the labor supply and the demand for goods produced in San Francisco remain unaffected, the market structure for goods produced in San Francisco would play a major role in determining the extent to which the lower local taxes would stimulate increased business activity in the city. Thus the five examples following indicate how the desire and ability to expand would vary from firm to firm.

Monopoly. If competition is limited in the local market, and the demand for the good is inelastic, the tax gain might not be passed on to the consumers. Even as the marginal cost curve falls in the long run the price would not fall by nearly as much as does the marginal cost (see Figure I). Hence very little expansion of output would be required to maximize profits, and the demand for business property would be little affected.

TAX CHANGE, MARKET STRUCTURE, PROFITS AND THE
DEMAND FOR BUSINESS PROPERTY: FIGURES I AND II

FIGURE I

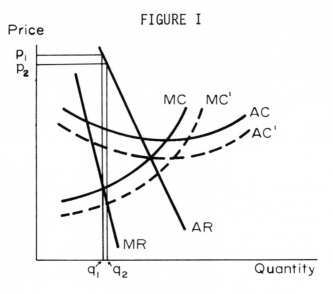

FIGURE II

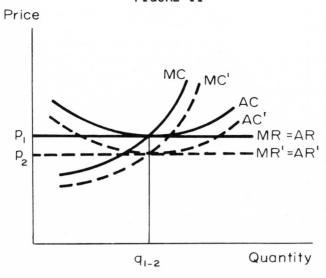

MC = Marginal Cost   MR = Marginal Revenue
AC = Average Cost   AR = Average Revenue

TAX CHANGE, MARKET STRUCTURE, PROFITS AND THE
DEMAND FOR BUSINESS PROPERTY: FIGURES III AND IV

FIGURE III

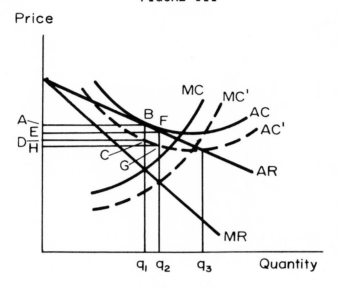

FIGURE IV

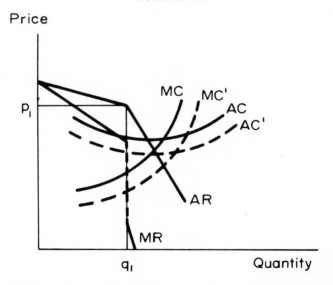

MC = Marginal Cost   MR = Marginal Revenue
AC = Average Cost   AR = Average Revenue

Pure competition. If competition, or potential competition, is intense, the producer would have to pass on his tax gain in order to maintain his competitive position in the local market. As his long-run cost curves drop, either old competitors or new entrants could easily attract his customers if price reductions do not follow (see Figure II). If the aggregate demand curve for these goods in San Francisco is elastic, the tax change might result in a significant increase in the production of these goods, with a resulting increase in the demand for business property.

Competition with imports. The local producer competing primarily with imported goods faces several alternatives depending on the elasticity of the demand schedule and on his own preference for sales or profit maximization. If demand is inelastic, the producer will behave like the monopolist in the first example above. As noted, demand for business property would be little affected.

But if the individual producer faces a very elastic demand schedule, he might expand his share of the local market by passing his tax reduction along to his customers. Or he might maintain prices and remain content with the same market share and larger after-tax profits. That is, the local firm could continue producing quantity q_1, its initial competitive position, and increase its economic profits from zero to ABCD (the reduction in the local tax bill). If the firm were a profit maximizer, it would set marginal cost equal to marginal revenue and increase output to quantity q_2, where profits would equal EFGH (see Figure III). Or, if the firm wished to maximize sales, it would increase output to quantity q_3 and continue to break even. In both of the latter two cases the demand for business property would increase.

National competition. The firm competing in the national market faces a similar choice between increasing its market share and remaining content with a constant share and higher after-tax profits. The structure of the national market would play an important role in its decision. A firm dominating the national scene and facing a very inelastic demand schedule, similar to the local monopoly in Figure I, would have equally little incentive to pass along any tax cut to its customers. If the industry is highly concentrated and interdependent, the local producer would accept the tax reduction in the form of higher profits: Cutting prices might stimulate price competition. Figure IV illustrates the case of the oligopolist facing a "kinky" demand curve. Like firms competing with foreign producers, the local firm facing a competitive national market could increase profits, market share, or both. Thus, whether demand for business property would be increased depends on the exact structure of the local market.

Summary. As shown above, the switch from property to income taxes would decrease the after-tax profits of those businesses with very high ratios of taxable income to taxable property, for their total local tax bill would increase as greater reliance was placed on income taxes. Taking market structure into account, we see that businesses competing only with other local businesses might find it possible to pass part of their increased tax bill on to consumers, even at the cost of some slackening of demand. The few firms dominant in the national market might also be able to pass on a sizable share of their increased taxes. But producers competing in national and international markets would probably find themselves in an uncomfortable position, forced to accept a reduction in their after-tax profits. Their demand for business property would, in fact, decrease.

Change in Demand for Goods and Services

As well as altering local tax bills, the imposition of an income tax would shift the demand for certain goods. The use of income taxes to lower property taxes would leave some individuals with higher after-tax money incomes, others with lower. Demand for goods and services purchased by the former groups would increase; demand for those purchased by the latter groups would decrease. The decrease could, in some cases, more than offset the fall in the local tax bill.

The Role of Wage Pressures

Take-home pay, real income and wage pressures. Imposition of an income tax would measurably increase the local taxes paid by many resident and nonresident wage earners. For evidence see Tables XVII and XX. The "real" well-being of these individuals would, of course, depend upon the degree to which benefits to business were shared with them. If the business tax decrease were shifted forward through lower prices, then both residents and nonresidents making purchases in San Francisco might not bear any additional tax burden as a result of the local income tax.

But there are several situations in which increased real income could not be expected. First, if residents own most of the city's production facilities and provide most of the labor, yet nonresidents make a large share of the purchases, residents might find that lower prices do little to offset their higher taxes. Second, businesses competing with producers located outside of San Francisco and facing an inelastic demand curve would have no incentive to reduce prices. The benefits of their reduced tax bills might go to stockholders and/or wage earners both in and outside San Francisco. To the extent that the stockholders and wage earners are San Franciscans, higher dividends and/or wages will partially offset the higher local taxes.

Nonresidents working in San Francisco and paying the local income tax would, in general, suffer from the local income tax. Only if lower prices or higher wages result from business's lower tax bills would part of their loss be offset. Lower prices may be an insignificant factor: first, because commuters do much of their shopping outside of San Francisco; and second, because only under competitive conditions would a San Francisco firm have any real incentive to lower its prices. Thus, a local tax levied on the earned income of nonresidents would lower both money and real incomes in all but the most unusual cases.[2]

Nonresidents could react to their lowered income in two ways: (1) by increasing their demands for higher wages; or (2) by moving out of the San Francisco labor market. Both reactions would tighten the labor market, leading to higher wages for those who stay. This development would increase the pressure on those firms with both a high taxable income/taxable property ratio and a large percentage of commuters in their work force. Even those firms that initially benefited from the income tax, but rely heavily on commuters as employees, might find their tax gain consumed by higher wages.

Residents would also be exerting pressure on wages. As will be shown in Chapter IV, even with a one percent net income tax imposed on all business income, the one percent tax on earned and unearned income of residents and the earned income of nonresidents would decrease the total tax payments of only those homeowners with annual incomes below $8000. With withholding imposed on earned income, even low-income residents would notice a definite reduction in take-home pay. Despite this, the wage pressure from residents would be less than that from nonresidents. First, residents owning property would benefit directly from the reduction of property taxes; second, residents would be more likely than commuters to benefit from price reductions resulting from the reduction of business property taxes. However, the pressure for higher wages from residents, though not as intense as that from nonresidents, would offset some of the benefits business had gained from lower tax bills.

Composition of the labor force. The higher wages demanded by commuters would hit especially hard at those businesses with many commuters in their labor force. For example, Table X indicates that in 1960, 61 percent of employees in San Francisco wholesale business, 51 percent of government employees, and 34 percent of employees in finance, insurance and real estate were commuters. In

TABLE X

PERCENT OF THE WORK FORCE COMMUTING TO WORK
IN SAN FRANCISCO ACCORDING TO TYPE OF BUSINESS, 1960

Type of business	Total employment	Percent residents	Percent commuters
Contract construction	21,000	73	27
Manufacturing	69,700	85	15
Transportation, communications and utilities	53,400	70	30
Wholesale trade	49,300	39	61
Retail trade	67,200	82	18
Finance, insurance and real estate	49,700	66	34
Service	92,200	88	12
Government	69,700	49	51

Source: U.S., Bureau of the Census, *Characteristics of Population, 1960*; and California, Department of Employment, *Community Labor Market Surveys*, 1960-61.

contrast, only 18 percent of retail employees, 15 percent of manufacturing employees, and 12 percent of service employees were commuters. The first group of businesses would be subjected to the strongest pressure for increasing wages.[3]

Like other factors noted in this discussion, wage pressures are cumulative in their effects. For example, if a firm operates in a highly competitive market, relies heavily on labor and draws upon commuters for a large share of its labor force, each of these factors would lessen San Francisco's desirability as a business location.

Elasticities in labor demand and supply. The elasticity of the firm's own demand for labor and the elasticity of the labor supply would be of major importance in determining how the tax change would affect any given enterprise.[4] With the elasticity of the supply curve between infinity and zero, a perfectly elastic demand curve for labor would place the entire burden of the wage tax upon laborers; a perfectly inelastic demand curve for labor would place the entire burden on employers or consumers. Similarly in the case of a labor supply curve with infinite elasticity and a labor demand curve with less than infinite elasticity, workers would not be burdened by the tax: It would be borne by employers or consumers.

At the other extreme is the case where the supply of labor is completely inelastic, and the demand for labor has an elasticity greater than zero. In this case the tax on wages would be borne entirely by the employees. Other things being equal, such firms would be least affected by the tax change under discussion. Of course the supply of labor will approach complete inelasticity only in the short run: Eventually workers will move elsewhere if conditions are more favorable. Allowing for time to adjust, the elasticity of both supply and demand curves for labor will lie between zero and infinity for all firms.

But labor supply and demand curves do not exist in isolation. Even a firm having a very elastic demand curve for labor and a very inelastic supply curve for labor could be forced to leave the city if the elasticity of the demand curve were derived from an extremely elastic demand curve for the final product. In this case, increases in the price of labor, no matter how small, could not be passed on to consumers. On the other hand, a highly inelastic demand curve for labor might be derived from a highly inelastic demand curve for the final product. In this case, the firm might be little affected by the rising wage level in the city, for it could pass higher wages on to consumers in the form of higher prices. As these examples indicate, one must go beyond simple elasticities of supply and demand for labor in order to ascertain which firms would be most adversely affected by the tax change.

The role of work incentives. Assuming constant prices, the imposition of a city income tax would reduce after-tax income from an additional hour's work. Hence additional leisure could be purchased at a lower price, for less income would be foregone. This effect, known as the substitution effect, occurs simultaneously with the so-called income effect. That is, low-income groups would experience higher after-tax money incomes (see Tables XVII and XX in Chapter IV). The combination of the two effects should lead to a reduction in the amount of work that low-income individuals are willing to supply. The higher income groups would experience a positive income effect, but the substitution effect with respect to their incentive to work would be negative.

This suggests that at existing wage rates those businesses employing low-income earners would have a smaller supply of labor available. To ensure an adequate supply, an increase in wages might be required. This pressure might, in turn, lead some businesses to relocate or to restrict their San Francisco operations, thus reducing the demand for certain types of business property.

In practice, however, there is little reason to believe that tax-induced alterations in work incentives would affect the supply of labor significantly. First, empirical evidence indicates that taxes have little effect on the amount of work people perform.[5] Second, since the local tax would be deductible from federal taxable income, its overall effect on income would be even smaller than the flat one percent rate would suggest. Third, prices would not remain constant. If lower property taxes led to price reductions in housing and other items influencing real income, the *real* cost of additional leisure might actually increase. However, the impact of a local tax on local prices is so uncertain that no prediction is hazarded as to whether the income effect on incentives to work would be negative or positive. Ignoring the price changes that might occur, Tables XVII and XX suggest that the income effect would in fact *increase* the incentive to work in all but the lowest income groups.

Conclusion

From the above analysis, it is clear that those businesses most likely to be adversely affected by a local income tax would be firms in a highly competitive market in which they would be forced to pass their tax savings along to consumers; firms whose work force is composed largely of commuters; firms whose demand for and supply of labor are very inelastic; and firms that produce goods primarily for those (high-income) individuals whose after-tax money income would drop because of the tax change.

All these factors interact with our earlier dichotomy between businesses with high and low taxable income/taxable property ratios. It is easy to imagine a manufacturer with a low taxable income/taxable property ratio, but very large payroll. Faced by workers seeking compensation for the additional tax being withheld from their take-home pay, such a manufacturer might find his property tax savings eroded by additional wage demands. Or a firm might have both a low taxable income/taxable property ratio and an inelastic supply of labor, yet be adversely affected by the tax because of a shift in the demand for its product or service.

It is clear that the tax change would affect the demand for business property. But in order to determine the exact change in demand, it would be necessary to examine the effect of the tax on the local tax bill of each business; its effect on the demand for the good or service produced; and its effect on the demand for and supply of each factor of production. Hence no overall conclusion can be drawn at the present time.

THE EFFECT OF TAX CHANGES
ON THE DEMAND FOR RESIDENTIAL PROPERTY

Factors Affecting the Demand
for Residential Property

It is somewhat easier to predict the effects of a local income tax on demand for residential property than for business property. Overall, the demand for low- and medium-income housing will probably increase in the long run, while demand for upper income housing will probably decline.

These changes are, for the most part, the product of altered levels of consumption. Employer withholding of the income tax, with its consequence of lower take-home pay for nearly all workers, might in itself decrease the level of consumption. But even more important, most middle-income groups and all higher income groups will pay a higher total tax bill to the city. (See Tables XVII and XX.) As a result of the tax change they would find that the overall cost of living in San Francisco had increased. The consequences for the demand for housing are detailed below.

Another factor that might affect the demand for housing is the possibility of capitalizing the property tax reductions permitted by the income tax. Such capitalization could create a further incentive to move from the city. Assume, for example, that prior to the city income tax Mr. Johnson owns a home with a market value of $25,000 and annual property taxes of $800. The city income tax permits the property tax to be reduced to $600. Assuming a 10 percent return on housing investment, Mr. Johnson's home has a market value of $27,000 after the tax reduction is capitalized. Mr. Johnson had previously wanted to live outside San Francisco, but could not afford to buy the equivalent suburban home priced at $26,000. He now finds that he can sell his city home and purchase a $27,000 suburban home. Even if his total city tax bill remains unchanged due to increased income taxes, the shift to an income tax might lead Mr. Johnson to move out of the city.[6]

Despite this, capitalization might not take place on a significant scale, for the property tax reduction is only one of the economic variables affecting the net return to property owners. The property tax reduction will result in a larger net return (the rise in the demand curve for housing from D_1 to D_2 illustrated in Figure V) only if other factors do not cancel its effects. But since other variables are in fact likely to cause shifts in the supply and demand curves, capitalization of tax reductions would probably not be fully realized.

A third factor affecting the demand for residential property is, of course, the construction industry's response to the tax change. Alterations in housing supply obviously play a major role in determining the returns for residential property investments. But at this time, attention will be focused on the demand side of the housing market.

The Demand for Rental Housing

Given existing conditions of supply and demand, there is little reason to expect that imposition of an income tax would promote any reduction in San Francisco rents. Hence the tax change would, in the short run, simply mean higher local tax bills for most renters. But the demand curve for rental property would have been affected. The reduction in renters' after-tax money income would bring about some decline in the demand for rental housing. Though demand for all types of rental housing would drop initially, the sharpest decline would occur in high-priced rental housing: High-income individuals would have the most to gain by moving from the city. Even in the short run this shift in the demand for high-income rental units might offset the landlord's gain from the property tax reduction. The landlord would have two options: He could either lower rents sufficiently to keep his high-income renters, or he could adapt his rental units for use by lower income renters. Either of these actions might cause his after-tax rental income

FIGURE V

REDUCTION IN PROPERTY TAXES AND THE DEMAND FOR HOMES AND RENTAL PROPERTY

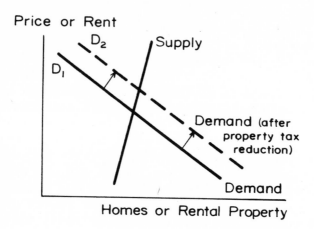

FIGURE VI

THEORETICAL DISTRIBUTION OF HOUSEHOLDS ACCORDING TO INCOME AND RENTS

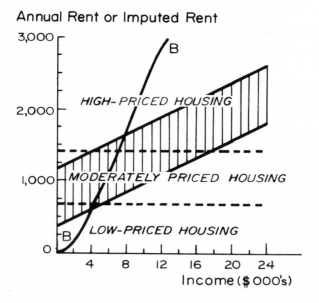

to be little above, or even below, its pre-income tax
level.

Low- and middle-income renters are not as mobile as
higher income groups, nor would they have as strong an
incentive to leave the city if an income tax were
imposed. This is important because, depending on the
form of tax employed, San Franciscans might be able to
escape the levy on unearned and/or earned income by
living outside the city. The number of households might
then shrink, as well as the average demand for housing
per household. Available data suggest that the number
of households with a high taxable income is relatively
large in San Francisco compared to many other cities.
County data (San Francisco is both a city and a county,
but comparable data for other cities are not available)
published by the California Franchise Tax Board indicate
that those with adjusted gross incomes (AGIs) over
$50,000 accounted for 10.3 percent of total AGI in San
Francisco in 1965. In San Diego and Los Angeles counties only 4.0 and 6.9 percent of total AGIs, respectively, were received by the same high-income group.[7]
Therefore, if high-income groups were to react strongly
against a local income tax by moving from the city, this
would have more impact on demand for housing in San
Francisco than in many other cities.

These two reasons--mobility and incentives--alone
make it unlikely that demand for low- and middle-income
rental units would decline as sharply as demand for
higher priced units. In addition some high-income individuals who previously occupied higher priced housing
might then be satisfied with moderately priced units.
Similarly some low-priced rental units would then be
rented to tenants who had previously been able to afford
moderately priced housing.

To summarize, we see that while the demand for all
types of rental housing would be likely to fall, rentals
catering to high-income individuals would experience
the sharpest decline. Thus high-priced rental units
would be subjected to the sharpest drop in market value.

In other words, the outward shift in the demand curve resulting from the property tax reduction might be more than offset by the movement of high-income groups from the city or by their decision to consume less housing.

In the long run the real estate market would adjust to this shift in demand by allocating relatively more resources to low-income units. The consequent reduction in rents might be such that low-income renters would actually benefit from the tax change. But this would not be true for most high-income renters. (See Table XX.)

The Demand for Housing by Homeowners and Renters Combined

Renters alone, of course, do not account for total housing demand: The demand of homeowners also plays a role. Figure VI helps illustrate how the housing demand of both these groups is affected by the tax change. The shaded area represents the distribution of expenditures for housing in each income class. The rents for homeowners are imputed, while those for renters are actual payments. As current income rises, so too do housing expenditures. In general, however, housing expenditures rise less rapidly than income.[8]

In Figure VI, the line BB represents the locus of break-even points for a particular type of local income tax. Each individual located above this line would have a lower local tax bill as a result of a given tax change; each individual below the line would have a higher total local tax bill. The tax bill of those on the line would be unchanged.

Finally, three types of housing are assumed to exist: low-priced (less than $700 annual net rent), moderately priced ($700-$1400 annual net rent), and high-priced (more than $1400 annual net rent).[9]

Viewing the hypothetical distribution in Figure VI, it appears that the large majority of those demanding low-priced housing would have higher after-tax money incomes. That is, their total local tax bill would decline. The majority of those demanding moderately priced housing would, however, experience a fall in their after-tax money income, and nearly all of those demanding high-priced housing would have lower after-tax money incomes. As a result, it is reasonable to expect that the demand curve for low-priced housing would rise. This result is illustrated in Figure VII. (It is assumed that within the range of the changes in after-tax money income, low-priced housing is not an inferior good.) Figure VIII indicates that the middle-income demand for moderately priced housing might fall slightly or remain about the same. Any overall fall would be lessened by (1) some previously low-priced housing consumers moving into the moderately priced category, and (2) some previously high-priced housing consumers dropping into the moderately priced category. And Figure IX shows that the demand for high-priced housing would fall.

Conclusion

The above analysis leads to the following conclusions concerning the demand for housing.

High-priced housing. High-income residents, whether homeowners or renters, would find that their after-tax money income had fallen considerably, and as a result they might consume less housing or move from the city. Either of these actions would decrease the demand for the high-priced housing that these groups had previously consumed.

Moderately priced housing. The precise change in demand for moderately priced housing would vary according to the type of local income tax enacted. Some forms of income tax would raise the after-tax income of most of the middle-income classes; other forms would lead to falling incomes for most of the group. However, the data presented in Chapter IV do seem to suggest that under most types of local income taxes middle-income groups

58

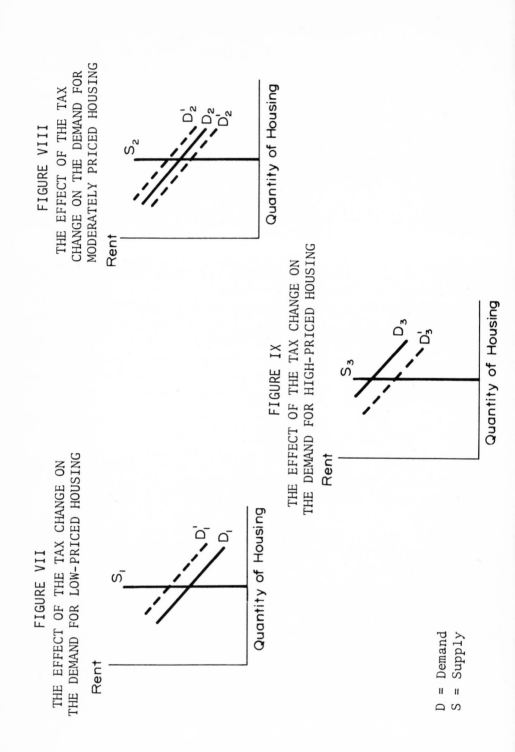

FIGURE VII

THE EFFECT OF THE TAX CHANGE ON
THE DEMAND FOR LOW-PRICED HOUSING

FIGURE VIII

THE EFFECT OF THE TAX
CHANGE ON THE DEMAND FOR
MODERATELY PRICED HOUSING

FIGURE IX

THE EFFECT OF THE TAX CHANGE ON
THE DEMAND FOR HIGH-PRICED HOUSING

D = Demand
S = Supply

would have higher after-tax incomes. This should be
reflected in the demand for housing and other commodi-
ties. And even if their incomes do fall, demand for
housing by middle-income groups will be supported by
increased demand for such units by tenants previously
occupying higher priced units.

Low-priced housing. The majority of low-income
homeowners would, under nearly all types of local income
taxes, experience a rise in their after-tax income. Thus
this group would increase its demand for both low-priced
and moderately priced housing. The increased rental
demand, however, would be concentrated in the moderately
priced range. As discussed before, the demand for low-
priced rental units would be little affected.

Thus, it does seem likely that in the long run the
demand for low- and moderately priced housing would
increase as a result of the imposition of a local income
tax. A decline in after-tax money incomes would not be
the only cause for this change: The movement of upper-
income residents from the city might also play a role.

THE EFFECT OF TAX CHANGES ON THE SUPPLY OF
BUSINESS AND RESIDENTIAL PROPERTIES

If demands were to remain unchanged, property
owners would find that the reduction in property taxes
left them with an increased net return on their investments. This increase would, in turn, lead to an increase
in construction. That is, the average and marginal net
return schedules on property investment would rise from
A and M to A' and M' in Figure X, leading to a construction investment increase from OS to OT.[10] But as noted
above, demand for business and residential property would
not remain unchanged. In some cases it would increase;
in others it would decline. Thus the net returns might
rise to only A" and M" or even fall to A'" and M'",
depending on the type of property. Only those holding
properties for which decreases in demand were offset by
property tax reductions would find themselves better off.

60

FIGURE X

THE EFFECT OF THE TAX CHANGE
ON CONSTRUCTION ACTIVITY

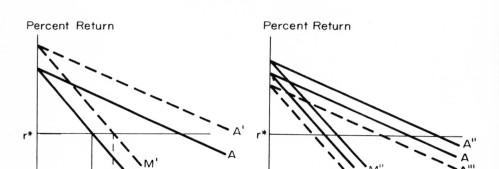

Percent Return

Percent Return

r*

r*

O

S   T

Outlay for Construction

A'

A

M'

M

A"

A

A'''

M'''   M   M"

Outlay for Construction

r* is the market rate of interest

And only in this case would there exist an incentive for
increased construction. Construction on other types of
property might be reduced despite property tax reductions.

The shifts in demand discussed above lead to the
following expectations concerning residential property:
(1) In the short run, the net return to low-price housing
might increase by more than the amount of the property
tax reduction. (2) The net return to moderately priced
housing might increase by more or less than the amount of
the tax reduction and would not be large in either direction. (3) The net return to high-priced housing would
rise by considerably less than the amount of the tax
reduction, and might even fall in the short run,
depending upon the income elasticity of the demand
for high-priced housing. Therefore, construction of

low-priced housing would be stimulated, as would conversion of formerly moderately priced units. It is uncertain how the tax change would affect the construction of moderately priced and high-priced housing.

A similar analysis applies to construction activity on business properties. Certain types of business may use less real property due to their higher total local tax bill, increased pressures for higher wages, or falling demand for their goods or services. Other businesses may demand more real property. As a result, some property owners would benefit from the tax change while others would suffer; construction of some types of property would be stimulated, while construction of other types would be depressed. However, the specific groups of people affected by these shifts in the demand curves cannot be determined, due to the lack of suitable data on property ownership.

EXPORTED EFFECTS OF A LOCAL INCOME TAX

The San Francisco economy has many links with Bay Area, state, national, and world economies. Thus tax changes affecting the city's economy have repercussions beyond its borders. For example, a tax on the income of San Francisco wage earners would lead to a fall in the supply of labor and higher before-tax wages in the city in the following manner: Fewer commuters would want to work in San Francisco; some residents would move out and work elsewhere.

At the same time, however, the emigrants from San Francisco would add to the labor supply outside the city, placing a slight downward pressure on the wage rate outside San Francisco. Such a fall in wage rates outside of the city would, of course, make it less attractive to leave the city. Like the increased before-tax wage levels in the city, this factor would help stem the exodus of labor. Even if wage rates outside the city did not fall, it might be more difficult to find positions at previously established wage rates. Finally, the rise in labor supply beyond the city's borders would, other things being equal, decrease the marginal productivity of additional labor. Thus workers outside of San Francisco would clearly be affected by tax policies pursued in the city.

A similar analysis is valid for capital. Because the markets of many San Francisco firms are located primarily outside the city, their demand conditions would not be affected by the imposition of an income tax. As a result, investment in capital goods would probably increase. There are two reasons why such an increase can be expected. First, the tax change would increase after-tax profits for many businesses, thus increasing the return on invested capital. This in itself would induce some businesses to expand their operations. Second, both the increasing returns to invested capital and the rising wage pressures discussed above would induce some businesses to substitute capital for labor. That is, the tax change would create an incentive to use more capital-intensive and less labor-intensive methods of production, even if the current level of operations were not expanded.

The increasing returns to capital in San Francisco, along with the adoption of more capital-intensive methods, would increase the capital imported to San Francisco and/or decrease the capital exported. This, in the long run, would lead to rising rates of return beyond San Francisco's borders due to the larger supply of capital within the city. In the short run, gross rates of return (before tax payments) would be lower in San Francisco than elsewhere, but net rates of return (after tax payments) would be higher. In the long run both gross and net rates of return to capital would be higher in areas outside San Francisco.

That the amount of capital or labor likely to be shifted into or out of San Francisco would be small rela- tive to the amount already outside, means that the city's impact on wages and rates of return may, in practice, be almost negligible. But the above analysis remains valid and must be recognized.

SUMMARY

The discussion at the beginning of this chapter pointed out that little attention has been devoted to the effects of a local income tax on resource allocation, and that most research has focused instead on income changes. It can now be seen that any analysis of the latter must also take into account changes in resource allocation.

It is, for example, clear that high-income groups have less desire than middle- and lower income groups to live in a city that has enacted a local flat-rate tax levied on both earned and unearned income. This distaste is increased if progressive tax rates are used. It follows therefore, that the investors, employees and suppliers connected with local establishments catering to high-income groups--the most exclusive restaurants, clubs, clothing stores, purveyors of costly entertainments and manufacturers of expensive articles--would probably suffer from the enactment of the local income tax. The factors that enter into the production of these goods and services would respond to a lowered demand, with results shown in lower wages, increased unemployment and lower returns to capital.

The effects on owners of residential property are less straightforward. If demand for housing remained constant, homeowners would be blessed with a capital gain due to property tax reduction. But in practice some influences would increase the demand for residential housing, while others would decrease it. The evidence suggests that those owning low- and moderately priced housing would, in general, experience some positive capital gain.

Whether owners of business property would benefit from a local income tax is even less clear cut. A reduction in property tax rates, other things being equal, would certainly be a windfall to business property owners. But some businesses would face a higher total tax burden and be unable to shift the increase. Others, with lower total local taxes, would have additional

options. The individual firm's total tax bill, market
structure, and wage pressures together determine the
desirability of its expanding within San Francisco,
moving into San Francisco, or moving out of San Francisco. These decisions in turn determine the effect of
the income tax on business property owners and on the
factors of production that business employs.

Those beyond the city borders who sell to firms
favored by the imposition of a local income tax would
themselves be favored. Conversely, those furnishing
goods and services to the businesses hurt by the local
income tax would themselves be hurt. The tax change
would also lead to slightly lower wages beyond the borders of San Francisco and to slightly higher returns to
capital.

NOTES TO CHAPTER III

1. "Michigan's First Local Income Tax," *National Tax Journal*, 15(4): 423-431 (1962).

2. Real income would fall less than money income if the tax change leads to lower prices in the city and subsequently, through competition, to lower prices in the suburbs.

3. This would be particularly true if only income earned in the city by residents and nonresidents was taxed.

4. Inelastic demand exists when changes in the price of labor stimulate little change in the quantity of labor demanded. Elastic demand exists when the quantity of labor demanded changes markedly relative to a change in the price of labor.

5. See George F. Break, "Income Taxes, Wage Rates, and the Incentive to Supply Labor Services," *National Tax Journal*, 6(4): 333-352 (1953); Break, "Income Taxes and Incentives to Work: An Empirical Study," *American Economic Review*, 47(5): 529-549 (1957); Robert Davidson, "Income Taxes and Incentive: The Doctor's Viewpoint," *National Tax Journal*, 6(3): 293-297 (1953); Thomas H. Sanders, *Effects of Taxation on Executives* (Boston: Harvard University Graduate School of Business Administration, 1951); and Robin Barlow, Harvey E. Brazer and James N. Morgan, "A Survey of Investment Management and Working Behavior among High Income Individuals," *American Economic Review*, 55(2): 252-264 (1965).

6. This type of movement may occur only in the short run. Given time, the rise in imputed net rentals will be followed by (1) increased demand for homes, (2) increased construction of homes, (3) a fall in imputed

net rentals, and (4) a fall in the capital gain the
homeowner can realize.

7. Adapted from California, Franchise Tax Board,
Annual Report, 1966, Table 6, "County Data By Adjusted
Gross Income Class," pp. 37-51.

8. For a discussion of housing expenditures as a
function of permanent rather than current income, see
Dick Netzer, Ch. II note 8, pp. 62-66. Housing expenditures appear to increase at least proportionately with
permanent income. Therefore, property taxes as a percent
of permanent income are proportional or even progressive.

9. An annual rent of $1400 would probably not
be considered high in present-day San Francisco; units
under $700 per year are practically nonexistent. But
these are the distinctions drawn by the 1960 U.S. Census,
which has provided data for this chapter.

10. See Ralph Turvey, *The Economics of Real Property*
(London: George Allen and Unwin, 1957), particularly pp.
10, 11 and 71.

IV

The Equity of Local Income Taxes

INTRODUCTION

The equity of state and local tax structures has long been a major concern of many economists. Most have focused on the tax structures' vertical equity, i.e., the equity of their treatment of persons with unequal resources. Table XI sets forth the results of some major research efforts in this direction. In 1964 California's state and local tax structure was regressive to the $15,000 (after-tax) income level. Similarly, Michigan's was regressive to the $10,000 level in 1956; Wisconsin's to the $7500 level in 1959. The Minnesota data are not directly comparable as they are based on current (before-tax) income: They indicate regressivity to the $5000 level in 1954. Such results lend substance to the claim that state and local tax structures are regressive over a broad range of incomes; that even when progressive federal income taxes are included, the overall vertical equity of the tax structure remains insufficient.

Other economists have concentrated on the question of horizontal equity, i.e., the equal treatment of individuals in equal circumstances. Taxation of property seldom complies with this condition, for the taxes are levied solely on the basis of the value of property owned or the value of property services consumed. They are not levied according to the taxpayer's overall economic position, thus discriminating against those who have a preference for property services.

TABLE XI

DISTRIBUTION OF THE BURDEN OF STATE AND LOCAL TAXES
IN CALIFORNIA, WISCONSIN, MICHIGAN AND MINNESOTA
AS A PERCENT OF INCOME BY INCOME CLASS

California, 1964[a]		Michigan, 1956[c]	
Income after federal income taxes	Taxes as percent of income	Money income after federal taxes	Taxes as percent of income
$ 0,000- 1,999	16.2	$ 0,000-1,999	23.84
2,000- 2,999	16.1	2,000-2,999	15.18
3,000- 3,999	15.8	3,000-3,999	12.39
4,000- 4,999	13.9	4,000-4,999	11.10
5,000- 5,999	13.1	5,000-6,999	9.48
6,000- 7,499	13.5	7,000-9,999	8.22
7,500- 9,999	12.1	10,000 & over	11.00
10,000-14,999	10.5		
15,000 & over	15.5		

Wisconsin, 1956[b]		Minnesota, 1954[d]	
Income after federal taxes	Taxes as percent of income	Current income	Taxes as percent of income
$ 0,000- 999	38.63	$ 0,000- 999	14.8
1,000-1,999	18.64	1,000-1,999	10.1
2,000-2,999	13.80	2,000-2,999	7.1
3,000-3,999	12.10	3,000-3,999	5.7
4,000-4,999	10.89	4,000-4,999	5.3
5,000-5,999	10.48	5,000-5,999	5.7
6,000-7,499	10.46	6,000-7,499	6.0
7,500-9,999	10.72	7,500-9,999	7.1
10,000 & over	15.05	10,000 & over	9.6

[a]See California, Assembly, Interim Committee on Revenue and Taxation, *Taxation of Property in California: A Major Tax Study, Part 5*, Vol. 4, No. 12 (1964). "State and Local Tax Burdens in California: The Property Tax Compared with State Taxes," by Levern P. Graves, pp. 32-53. See esp. p. 46, as basis for the table above.

[b]*Wisconsin's State and Local Tax Burden: Impact, Incidence and Tax Revision Alternatives* (Madison, Wisconsin: University of Wisconsin Tax Study Committee, 1959). See p. 65 as basis for the table above.

[c]Derived from Richard A. Musgrave and Darwin W. Daicoff, "Who Pays the Michigan Taxes?" in *Michigan Tax Study: Staff Papers* (Lansing, Michigan: 1958), pp. 131-183. See esp. p. 140.

[d]O.H. Brownlee, "Estimated Distribution of Minnesota Taxes and Public Expenditure Benefits," *Studies in Economics and Business No. 21* (Minneapolis: University of Minnesota Press, 1960), p. 4.

Due to the attacks on the vertical and horizontal
inequity of existing state and local taxes, there has
been a renewed search for sources of state and local
revenues that would meet rising expenditures and at the
same time improve the overall equity of the tax structure. To attain these goals several large cities and
many smaller ones have instituted local income taxes.
*How, then, will the adoption and increased use of local
income taxes affect the equity of a local tax structure?*
This is a key question in the present study.

Most economists have assumed that local income taxes
will, in fact, increase the equity of the local tax
structure. Studies comparing the formal incidence of
property taxes and local income taxes have found that a
flat-rate tax levied on earned income would be considerably more progressive than a real estate tax.[1] Similarly, there can be little doubt that a local income tax
levied as a percentage of state income tax liability
would be progressive in those states having progressive
income taxes. Given the regressivity consistently found
in studies of the property tax, supplements to progressive state income taxes would probably be more progressive than the property tax.[2]

However, this chapter and those following demonstrate that a movement toward local income taxes may be
less equitable than is commonly believed. The study
first examines the way the treatment of individuals in
different positions differs under the existing property
tax system, and how treatment would differ under a
variety of forms of local income taxes.

Throughout this examination of the equity of local
income taxes, two major assumptions have been made consistently:

> (1) When an income tax is levied,
> property tax rates are lowered
> in order that the total municipal
> revenues remain unchanged.

(2) The change in the tax structure
has no effect on municipal expenditures.

These assumptions make it possible to hold public expenditures constant and to avoid the inflationary or deflationary effects accompanying expenditure changes. It might be more realistic to assume instead that property tax rates would increase more slowly with than without a local income tax. But this assumption's contribution to reality is more than offset by the increased complexities it would add to the analysis.[3]

This analysis of the equity of local income taxes does not attempt to answer the question of how the taxation of individuals in different circumstances should differ. For the economist to contribute to this judgment it would be necessary to introduce interpersonal utility comparisons that he is not uniquely qualified to make. This study of equity therefore goes no further than laying the evidence before policymakers.

The evidence concerning the distributional effects of a local income tax in the City of San Francisco is particularly relevant, for in recent years San Francisco has seriously considered the adoption of some form of local income tax in response to pressure from residential property owners faced with rapidly rising property taxes.[4] In fact, property taxes paid by many homeowners more than doubled between 1966 and 1968. But although the findings of this study are based on San Francisco data, the method of analysis and the general conclusions can be applied to any city planning to use an income tax to relieve the pressure on property taxes.

FACTORS DETERMINING REVENUE
FROM LOCAL INCOME TAXES

In order to evaluate the possible impact of a local income tax on the equity of the San Francisco tax structure, it is essential to estimate the revenue-raising potential of this form of taxation. How much of a reduction in other types of revenues will income tax funds permit? The revenues raised will depend upon a number of factors: Are nonresidents to be taxed, and if so, at what rates? Does the central city have priority in taxing earnings of both commuters and residents? What exemptions, deductions and credits are to be allowed in calculating tax liability? Is the unearned income of residents to be taxed? Are business net profits to be taxed? What structure of tax rates is to be utilized?

Nonresidents as a Source of Revenue

Estimates projected from 1960 census data indicate that 442,000 individuals were employed in San Francisco in 1967. Of these, approximately 126,000, or 28.5 percent, were commuters. (See Table XII.) The income these commuters earned in San Francisco is estimated at $913 million (see Table XIII). The importance of revenues raised through the taxing of commuters would, of course, vary from city to city (see Appendix B for this chapter).

The Right to Tax

Another crucial issue concerns which jurisdiction has priority in taxing earned income. For example, a state statute gives Philadelphia the right to tax the full earnings of commuters who work in Philadelphia but reside elsewhere.[5] Pittsburgh does not have the same power. Hence, Pittsburgh can tax the earnings of in-commuters only to the extent that the tax rate in the place of residence is below one percent, while Philadelphia levies its full 2 percent rate on the earnings of in-commuters. As a result of these legal characteristics, Philadelphia derives a larger percentage of its municipal income taxes from nonresidents, though the share of commuters in Pittsburgh's work force (33.3 percent) is much larger than in Philadelphia (22.0 percent). In 1954 nonresidents contributed 15 percent to income tax revenues in Philadelphia and 10 percent in Pittsburgh.[6]

TABLE XII

COMMUTERS INTO SAN FRANCISCO IN 1967[a]

1.	Estimated population	747,500
2.	Total number employed in San Francisco	441,974
3.	Number living *and* working in San Francisco	316,038 (71.5%)
4.	Number of workers living in San Francisco	339,629
5.	Number commuting into the city, (2 - 3).	125,936 (28.5%)
6.	Number commuting out of the city, (4 - 3).	23,591

[a]See Appendix A for estimation procedures and notes.

Philadelphia, New York City, Louisville and St. Louis have all protected the revenue-raising powers of their local income taxes by disallowing tax credits for income taxes paid to other local jurisdictions. However, some form of compromise, formal or informal, is usually concluded between the central city and adjoining communities. Such an agreement typically provides that each will receive some income tax revenue from individuals living in one jurisdiction but working in another. Arrangements of this type exist among all Michigan cities imposing income taxes and among some Ohio cities.[7]

Exemptions and Deductions

Exemptions and deductions can also play a crucial role in determining the size of the tax base. A basic exemption of $600 for the worker and each of his dependents would reduce the tax base by about 20 percent in San Francisco. Deductions, as defined by California personal income tax law, would reduce the tax base by another 20 percent. While they would erode close to 40 percent of the tax base, deductions and exemptions would

TABLE XIII

TYPES OF LOCAL INCOME TAXES AND THEIR REVENUE POTENTIAL IN SAN FRANCISCO IN 1967

Type:

I   A 1 percent levy on both earned and unearned income of San Francisco residents and on the income of nonresidents earned in San Francisco.

II   A 1 percent levy on the earned income of San Francisco residents and on the income of nonresidents earned in San Francisco.

III   A 1 percent levy on all income earned in San Francisco. This excludes income that San Francisco residents earn outside of San Francisco.

IV   A 1 percent tax on both earned and unearned income of San Francisco residents.

V   A 1 percent tax on the earned income of residents alone.

VI   A Type I tax plus a 1 percent tax on all corporate income.

VII   A Type I tax plus a 1 percent tax on all business income.

VIII   A Type I tax plus a 3 percent tax on all corporate income.

IX   A Type I tax plus a 3 percent tax on all business income.

X   A local income tax levied as a 50 percent supplement to the state personal income tax.

XI   A Type II tax plus a 1 percent tax on all business income.

(1) Type of tax	(2) Residents' earned income[a]	(3) Residents' unearned income[b]	(4) Earned income of in-commuters[c]	(5) Corporate income[d]	(6) Other business income[e]	(7) Earned income of out-commuters[f]	(8) Tax revenue estimate	Reduction in tax base resulting from $600 per dependent exemption	
								(9) Value of exemptions[g]	(10) Reduction in tax base due to exemptions
	(000's)	(000's)	(000's)	(000's)	(000's)	(000's)	(000's)	(000's)	(percent)
I	2,069,000	506,000	913,000	-	-	-	34,870	631,303	18.1
II	2,069,000	-	913,000	-	-	-	29,820	631,303	21.2
III	2,069,000	-	913,000	-	-	(-145,000)	28,370	599,740	21.1
IV	2,069,000	506,000	-	-	-	-	25,750	448,500	17.4
V	2,069,000	-	-	-	-	-	20,690	448,500	21.7
VI	2,069,000	506,000	913,000	461,000	-	-	39,490	631,303	16.0
VII	2,069,000	506,000	913,000	461,000	229,000	-	41,780	631,303	15.1
VIII	2,069,000	506,000	913,000	461,000	-	-	48,710	631,303	13.0
IX	2,069,000	506,000	913,000	461,000	229,000	-	55,580	631,303	11.4
X	-	-	-	-	-	-	23,000	-	-
XI	2,069,000	-	913,000	461,000	229,000	-	36,720	631,303	17.2

For notes a, b, c, d, e, f, g, see Appendix C, "Calculations for Table XIII."

make the overall tax structure more progressive, as well as more equitable on the basis of ability to pay. The need for revenues, the desire to keep local income tax rates at nominal levels, and the desire to simplify administration, compliance and enforcement have prevented most of the local income tax jurisdictions from allowing either deductions or exemptions. However, New York City, Baltimore, and cities in Michigan have included such provisions in their local income tax frameworks.8

San Francisco's Potential Tax Base

The types of income that might be included in the San Francisco tax base are listed in columns (2) to (6) of Table XIII, along with the magnitude of each type. The categories include earned and unearned income of residents, earned income of nonresidents, and both corporate and noncorporate business income. From these figures it can be seen that the inclusion of nonresident income, unearned income of residents, and business income more than doubles the tax base, raising it from less than $2.1 billion to around $4.2 billion. The exclusion of nonresident earned income alone would reduce the tax base by about 22 percent.

Column (8) of Table XIII provides estimates of the revenues that would have been raised in 1967 by each of 11 selected forms of local income tax. For example, using a one percent flat-rate tax, revenue estimates range from $20.7 million when only the earned income of residents is taxed to $41.8 million when earned nonresident income and business income are also taxed. If corporate income were taxed at 3 percent, revenues would rise to $48.7 million.9 'The table also indicates that a 50 percent supplement to the state personal income tax would have raised $23 million in San Francisco in 1967.

THE PROGRESSIVITY OF LOCAL INCOME
AND PROPERTY TAXES COMPARED

In the City of San Francisco property taxes on both homeowners and renters appear to be highly regressive. Table XIV indicates that for homeowners property taxes ranged from 14.7 to 2.7 percent of total income for those having incomes of $2000 to $35,000, respectively. (This regressivity is slightly reduced, as Appendix F shows, when imputed rentals, minus ownership expenses, are included in income.) Table XV indicates that for renters the range over the same income spread was 5.0 to 0.6 percent.

In contrast to this regressivity, Table XVI demonstrates that each type of income tax appears to be progressive. The exclusion of certain types of income from taxation--unemployment and Social Security benefits, private pensions and retirement benefits, public social assistance and private relief, and military allotments and pensions--accounts for the progressivity of these flat-rate taxes.

Considering the progressivity of the income tax and the regressivity of the property tax, one would expect that a shift from property taxation to income taxation would benefit low-income homeowners more than the high-income homeowners. But because business property owners receive 52 percent of the benefit from any property tax reduction in San Francisco, further analysis is necessary to ascertain how many homeowners and renters would actually benefit from the property tax reductions made possible by income tax revenues.

HOMEOWNERS AND THE EQUITY
OF A LOCAL INCOME TAX

Table XVII indicates the change in local tax payments that homeowners could expect on the average if local income tax revenues were used to reduce property taxes. For each type of local income tax examined, those

TABLE XIV

PROPERTY TAXES AS A PERCENT OF MONEY INCOME
FOR HOMEOWNERS IN SAN FRANCISCO IN 1967

Money income before taxes	Property tax payment	Assessed value	Tax as a percent of income
$ 2,064	$303	$ 3,443	14.7
3,354	328	3,727	9.8
4,902	292	3,318	6.0
6,450	364	4,136	5.6
7,804	393	4,466	5.0
9,675	455	5,148	4.7
12,642	485	5,511	3.8
17,415	607	6,898	3.5
35,217	944	10,727	2.7

Source: See Appendix D, Part I.

homeowners in the high-income classes would pay more into
the city coffers than previously, while those with low
incomes would pay less. The supplement to the state
income tax, due to its progressive rates, would hit the
very high-income groups hardest, thus reducing the
regressivity of the local tax structure more than any
other form of local income tax. But whatever the type
employed, the vertical equity of the local tax structure
would be improved for homeowners.

The lower part of Table XVII shows the "net savings
after federal tax deductions." For example, column (5)
indicates that if the revenues from a Type I local income
tax were used to reduce property taxes, the four lowest
income classes of homeowners would, on the average,
receive increased after-tax money incomes. On the other
hand, the five highest income classes would receive
smaller after-tax money incomes. Columns (6) through
(15) indicate the net savings if other forms of local
income taxes were adopted. The pattern of net savings
indicates that, whatever the type of local income tax

TABLE XV

SAN FRANCISCO PROPERTY TAX BURDEN ON RENTERS
ACCORDING TO INCOME CLASS, 1967-68

(1)	(2)	(3)	(4)	(5)	(6)	(7)
Money income before taxes	Average annual rent[a]	Value of rented property	Assessed value	Total property taxes paid	Tenant's share	Tenant's share of taxes as a percent of income
$ 2,064	$ 569	$ 5,989	$1,461	$129	$103	5.0
3,354	719	7,568	1,847	163	130	3.9
4,902	795	8,368	2,042	180	144	3.0
6,450	903	9,505	2,319	204	163	3.6
7,804	905	9,526	2,324	205	164	2.1
9,675	983	10,347	2,525	222	178	1.8
12,642	1,049	11,042	2,694	237	190	1.5
17,415	1,192	12,547	3,061	269	215	1.2
35,217	1,086	11,432	2,789	245	196	0.6

[a]The average rental payments by each of the four highest money income classes appear to be inexplicably low. Though no improved method of estimation is readily apparent, these rental figures and the resulting high regressivity of the property tax on renters may be viewed with some skepticism.

Source: See Appendix D, Part II.

TABLE XVI

THE EFFECTIVE RATE OF VARIOUS LOCAL
INCOME TAXES IN SAN FRANCISCO FOR 1967

(1)	(2)	(3)	(4)	(5)	(6)	(7)
Money income before taxes[a]	Taxes paid on earned income only[b]	Taxes paid on earned plus unearned income[c]	50% supplement[d]	(2)/(1)	(3)/(1)	(4)/(1)
	(Types II, III,V,XI)	(Types I,IV,VI, VII,VIII,IX)	(Type X)	%	%	%
$ 2,064	$ 5	$ 7	0	.24	.34	.0
3,354	19	22	0	.57	.65	.0
4,902	35	40	0	.71	.82	.0
6,450	53	57	1	.82	.88	.0
7,804	68	73	12	.87	.94	.2
9,675	89	94	44	.92	.97	.5
12,642	116	124	90	.92	.98	.7
17,415	155	168	195	.89	.96	1.1
35,217	306	352	1,141	.87	1.00	3.2

[a] Bureau of Labor Statistics data are adjusted to 1967 income levels (see Appendix D, Part I).

[b] Earned income includes wages and salaries, rents and food received as pay, self-employment income, income from roomers and boarders, minus occupational expenses.

[c] Includes earned income, net rents, interest, dividends.

[d] See Appendix E.

employed, the vertical equity of the local tax structure would be improved for homeowners.

In addition to improving the vertical equity of the local tax system, previous studies indicate that the horizontal equity of income taxes far surpasses that of property taxes.[10] This holds whether the property tax is viewed as an ability-to-pay levy or as a benefits-received levy.

RENTERS AND THE EQUITY OF A LOCAL INCOME TAX

If all individuals were homeowners, a local income tax could clearly improve the equity of a local tax system. But many households, particularly in large cities, rent their dwelling space. In 1960, 65 percent of all households in San Francisco were renters (Table XVIII). As noted in Table XV, the property tax payments made directly by renters are regressive. This fact, combined with the progressivity of the income taxes being considered, could reasonably lead to the conclusion that for renters, too, the local tax system would become less regressive with the introduction of an income tax. However, it is theoretically possible for a tax change to have a progressive influence on the tax structure for each of two separate groups, and yet to have a regressive influence when these two groups are combined. Therefore, the impact of the tax change on renters alone must be more carefully examined, and the impact on homeowners and renters combined must be examined, before such a conclusion can be reached.

Renters and Vertical Equity--The Short Run

Utilizing partial equilibrium analysis we would expect the imposition of a local income tax to lower rents in the short run. The "short run" is known to students of real estate markets as the "standing stock" period, i.e., the period in which no construction can occur. Therefore, the supply curve of available housing

TABLE XVII

THE NET BURDEN ON SAN FRANCISCO RESIDENT-HOMEOWNERS OF LOCAL INCOME TAXES OF VARIOUS TYPES WHEN THE INCOME TAX REVENUES ARE USED TO REDUCE PROPERTY TAXES[a]

(1) Money income before taxes[c]	Income tax payment[b,d]			Property tax savings[b,e]										
	(2) Types I,IV, VI,VII, VIII,IX	(3) Types II,III, V,XI	(4) Type X	(5) I	(6) II	(7) III	(8) IV	(9) V	(10) VI	(11) VII	(12) VIII	(13) IX	(14) X	(15) XI
$ 2,064	$ 7	$ 5	$ 0	$ 55	$ 47	$ 45	$ 41	$ 32	$ 63	$ 66	$ 77	$ 88	$ 36	$ 58
3,354	22	19	0	60	51	49	44	35	68	72	83	95	39	63
4,902	40	35	1	53	45	43	39	31	60	64	74	85	35	56
6,450	57	53	12	66	56	54	49	39	75	80	92	106	44	70
7,804	73	68	44	72	61	58	53	42	81	86	100	114	47	76
9,675	94	89	90	82	70	67	61	48	94	99	115	132	54	89
12,642	124	116	195	88	75	72	65	52	100	106	123	141	58	93
17,415	168	155	1,141	110	94	90	81	65	126	133	154	177	73	117
35,217	352	306		172	146	140	127	101	195	207	240	275	113	182

Net savings after federal tax deductions[f]

(1) Money income before taxes[c]	(5) I	(6) II	(7) III	(8) IV	(9) V	(10) VI	(11) VII	(12) VIII	(13) IX	(14) X	(15) XI
2,064	48	42	40	34	27	56	59	70	81	30	53
3,354	32	27	44	18	13	38	42	51	61	33	37
4,902	11	8	7	-1	-3	17	20	28	37	29	17
6,450	7	2	1	-6	-11	15	19	28	37	37	14
7,804	-1	-5	-8	-16	-21	6	11	22	33	28	6
9,675	-9	-15	-17	-26	-33	0	4	17	30	8	0
12,642	-28	-32	-34	-45	-50	-19	-14	-1	13	-25	-18
17,415	-44	-46	-49	-65	-64	-32	-26	-60	7	-92	-28
35,217	-108	-96	-100	-136	-123	-94	-87	-67	-46	-556	-64

a These tables do not take into account the effects of price changes resulting from changes in taxes paid by business.

b Though income tax payments by a family may be identical under two or more types of local income taxes, the property tax savings differ due to variations in the income tax base. For example, a tax base that includes business income would permit a larger reduction in property tax rates than one excluding business income.

c See Appendix D, Part I.

d (BLS Report No. 237-37), *Consumer Expenditures and Income, Urban Places in the Western Region, 1960-61* (1964), gives for each income class the share of income composed of public unemployment and Social Security benefits, private pensions and retirement, public social assistance and private relief, and military allotments and pensions. These forms of income are assumed to be nontaxable with the remaining part of money income assumed to be taxable. Dividends, interest, capital gains and rents are the primary sources of unearned income. Though the income of each class has increased, it is assumed that the taxable income remains the same percentage of each class. A one percent tax rate is applied to the remaining income.

e A tax of the form suggested in Type I would have yielded $34,870,000 in 1967. The estimated yield of the 8.80 tax rate to be applied was $191 million (*Controller's Annual Report of Assessed Valuation and Tax Rates of the Counties of California* for the fiscal year, 1967-68). The $34,870,000 tax revenue would have permitted a reduction in tax rate to $7.19 which would have resulted in "Property tax savings" as shown.

f Local income and property taxes are deductible from taxable income for federal tax purposes; hence the savings are less after allowing for this adjustment. The tax rate applicable to each AGI level is obtained from *Statistics of Income: Individual Income Tax Returns, 1965*, Table 21 (U.S., Department of the Treasury, Washington, D.C.: 1968), p. 56.

TABLE XVIII

PERCENT OF OCCUPIED DWELLING UNITS THAT WERE RENTED IN 30 CITIES IN 1960

New York City	78.3	Columbus	48.3
Newark	77.4	San Diego	47.3
Boston	72.7	Minneapolis	47.3
Washington, D.C.	70.0	Louisville	46.7
Chicago	65.7	Denver	46.5
San Francisco	65.0	Kansas City, Mo.	46.2
New Orleans	62.4	Baltimore	45.7
St. Louis	61.8	Memphis	44.8
Cincinnati	59.6	Indianapolis	44.7
Buffalo	55.7	Seattle	42.6
Cleveland	55.1	Detroit	41.8
Atlanta	54.4	Dallas	40.3
Los Angeles	53.8	Houston	39.6
Milwaukee	51.6	Philadelphia	38.1
Pittsburgh	51.2	San Antonio	36.4

Source: U.S. Bureau of the Census, *1960 Census of Housing: Metropolitan Housing*, Vol. II (1-7), compiled from Tables B6, C6 and D6.

remains much the same before and immediately after the tax change. Normal demand and supply analysis leads to the conclusion that rents would remain unchanged unless the demand curve shifted. But renters, faced with an additional income tax, would have lower after-tax incomes. Thus they would cut back spending on all goods and services, including housing, and a slight fall in demand (leftward shift in the demand curve) for housing would occur. Normal demand and supply analysis thus suggests that renters, though faced with another income tax, would also find rents lower.

Unfortunately for renters, empirical studies contradict this conclusion. With a slight fall in the demand for rental housing, the price of rental housing "acts as though" the supply of rental housing were infinitely elastic over the relevant market range.[11] The reduction in the demand for housing may not be considered permanent, and rather than reducing rents, landlords are willing to accept a temporary increase in their vacancy rates. This is particularly true of multiunit rental housing where lowering rents to fill vacancies may decrease total revenues. Increased vacancy rates are also tolerated more easily when the initial occupancy rates were high. In this case any fall in demand is more likely to be considered temporary.[12]

Thus it appears that the shift in demand stemming from imposition of a local income tax would have little effect on rents during the standing stock period. Most renters would find that the tax change had simply resulted in higher local taxes. But due to the progressive nature of the income taxes, total local taxes on renters as a group would be less regressive than they had been previously.

Renters and Vertical Equity--The Long Run

Given that renters would suffer from the tax change in the short run, what would be their fortune over the "construction period," i.e., a period sufficiently long for the housing stock to vary? Note first that, other things being equal, owners of rental property would find that the reduction in property taxes left them with an increased net return on their investments, for any fall in demand would probably not cause rents to decrease by the full amount of the property tax reduction. This increase in return would lead to an increase in construction activity. With an increase in the demand for building sites the costs of such sites--assuming unchanged interest rates--would rise.[13] Assuming that construction costs do not increase in proportion to net rents after property taxes, the rate of return would rise above its previous level.[14] This increased profitability in rental housing would lead to more extensive and intensive land development. But with the consequent increase in accommodations available, rents would fall

TABLE XIX

PERCENT OF THE TOTAL NUMBER OF OCCUPIED RENTAL UNITS
THAT ARE IN STRUCTURES HAVING FIVE OR MORE UNITS,
FOR THE 31 LARGEST CITIES IN THE UNITED STATES

New York City	77.9	San Diego	28.8
San Francisco	59.8	St. Louis	28.7
Washington, D.C.	58.7	Pittsburgh	28.4
Seattle	57.5	Milwaukee	28.0
Chicago	54.9	Philadelphia	27.2
Kansas City, Mo.	51.9	Columbus	26.0
Newark	47.1	Dallas	25.3
Minneapolis	46.9	New Orleans	23.7
Los Angeles	44.9	Louisville	23.5
Boston	44.3	Buffalo	22.1
Denver	43.7	Memphis	21.4
Cincinnati	36.9	Houston	18.4
Detroit	35.8	Baltimore	16.4
Atlanta	34.5	San Antonio	14.8
Cleveland	31.2	Phoenix	13.0
Indianapolis	29.9		

Source: See note for Table XVIII.

below the level that would exist if no tax change had occurred. Renters would begin to benefit from the reduction in property taxes.

As noted in the discussion of short-run behavior, vacancy rates would have to rise to some (unknown) level before rents would begin to decline. This should hold true for vacancies created by new construction as well as for those created by decreases in demand. Thus some construction would have to be completed before rents would begin to decline. The exact amount, however, remains uncertain.

In a city such as San Francisco, in which multiunit structures comprise the bulk of current and future housing, the supply of housing tends to increase more slowly than in communities relying heavily on single-unit structures. E.M. Fisher has explained that:

> [C]onstruction of dwellings for rent
> increases rapidly as the evidence that
> rents will continue to rise becomes
> more convincing. The increase seems
> likely to appear first in the smaller
> types of structure--two-, three-, four-
> family buildings.... it appears that
> the building of large multi-family
> structures does not achieve great
> volume until a seller's market has
> prevailed long enough to have produced
> a considerable rise in rents.[15]

As Table XIX indicates, a relatively high percent of rental units in San Francisco are located in large structures.

Although relatively little is known about the speed with which the supply of housing can adapt to a change in demand, Richard F. Muth's study makes possible some useful predictions. Muth found that:

>...even though new construction is
>highly responsive to changes in demand
>conditions for housing, we have seen
>that the lag in the adjustment of
>actual housing stock to the level ulti-
>mately desired is also quite substan-
>tial. We estimated that individuals
>seek to add about one-third of the
>difference between actual and desired
>stock to the housing stock in any year.
>This, in turn, implies that, for a
>given adjustment to be 90 per cent com-
>pleted, about six years are required.[16]

This suggests that investors need time to adjust the gap
between the existing and desired levels of housing owned.
Muth's findings further support the assertion that it may
take several years for renters to receive any significant
benefits from the property tax reduction.

Thus, the final position of renters depends upon
three groups of factors. First is the length of time it
takes the housing market to respond to reductions in
property taxes. If this response takes several years,
renters may suffer from local income taxes without any
offsetting benefit for a considerable period of time.
Second, the stronger the tenant's position relative to
the landlord's, the better off the tenant will be. This
depends on (a) the cost and bother of moving, (b) the
difficulty and expense of arranging alternative accommodations, and (c) the difficulty and costs to the landlord
of finding another tenant. Third, the percentage of
their incomes that renters spend on housing is significant. Those with high incomes and modest tastes in
housing would suffer relatively more than any other
group: Their incomes would drop most without compensation in the form of lower rents.

The Effects on the Long-Run
After-Tax Income of Renters

To ascertain the overall effects of the local income tax on the after-tax income of renters, it is assumed that landlords would receive 20 percent of the benefit from any property tax reduction, i.e., the share falling on land. It is further assumed that the property tax reduction would eventually be passed on to renters. On the basis of these assumptions Table XX gives the approximate benefits that would accrue to renters in various income classes from 11 types of local income taxes considered. It appears that in most cases only the lowest income classes of renters would benefit from the tax change even in the long run. Renters with higher incomes and extremely high housing expenditures relative to income might also benefit. But even for those with low incomes it might take years to recoup the short-run losses resulting from the income tax. Most renters in middle- and high-income classes would pay increased local taxes in both the long and short run. These findings hold for 10 of the 11 forms of local income tax examined in this study. The only exception is the tax levied as a percent of the state income tax liability. But even in this case the four highest income classes of renters would suffer a net loss. See column (14) of Table XX.

Compared to homeowners, then, renters would be affected adversely by the imposition of a local income tax. If high-income groups tend to be homeowners while low-income groups tend to be renters, a careful analysis should precede conclusions as to whether the partial replacement of property tax revenues by income tax revenues would add to the progressivity of the tax system. As a first step toward this analysis it is necessary to examine the distribution of homeowners and renters by income classes.

Who Rents?

U.S. census data for San Francisco in 1960 indicate that 78 percent of all family units with incomes below

TABLE XX

THE NET BURDEN ON SAN FRANCISCO RESIDENT-RENTERS OF LOCAL INCOME TAXES OF VARIOUS TYPES
WHEN THE INCOME TAX REVENUES ARE USED TO REDUCE PROPERTY TAXES

| (1) | Income tax payment[a] | | | Property tax savings[a] | | | | | | | | | | |
| | (2) Types I,IV, VI,VII, VIII,IX | (3) Types II,III, V,XI | (4) Type X | (5) I | (6) II | (7) III | (8) IV | (9) V | (10) VI | (11) VII | (12) VIII | (13) IX | (14) X | (15) XI |
Money income before taxes														
$ 2,064	$ 7	$ 5	$ 0	$ 19	$ 16	$ 15	$ 14	$ 11	$ 22	$ 22	$ 26	$ 30	$ 12	$ 20
3,354	22	19	0	24	20	19	18	14	27	29	34	38	16	25
4,902	40	35	0	26	22	22	19	15	30	31	37	42	17	28
6,450	57	53	1	30	26	24	22	18	34	36	42	47	20	31
7,804	73	68	12	30	26	25	22	18	34	36	42	48	20	32
9,675	94	89	44	33	28	26	24	19	37.	39	46	52	22	34
12,642	124	116	90	34	30	28	26	21	39	42	48	55	23	37
17,415	168	155	195	39	34	32	29	23	45	47	55	62	26	41
35,217	352	306	1,141	39	30	30	26	21	41	43	50	57	24	37
				Net savings after federal tax deductions										
2,064				12	11	10	7	6	15	13	19	23	10	15
3,354				2	1	0	-3	-4	4	6	10	14	13	5
4,902				-12	-11	-11	-17	-16	-8	-7	-3	2	14	-6
6,450				-22	-22	-24	-27	-29	-19	-17	-12	-8	17	-17
7,804				-35	-34	-35	-42	-41	-32	-30	-25	-20	6	-29
9,675				-49	-49	-51	-56	-56	-46	-43	-39	-34	-18	-45
12,642				-72	-65	-67	-78	-76	-68	-64	-61	-55	-52	-62
17,415				-97	-91	-93	-104	-99	-92	-94	-85	-80	-127	-86
35,217				-188	-166	-166	-196	-177	-187	-185	-181	-177	-670	-161

[a]See note b, Table XVII.

$3000 were renters. The same percentage holds for all family units with incomes below $5000. But only 39 percent of those families with incomes above $10,000 rented their housing. Thus as Figures XI and XII illustrate, renters are concentrated heavily in the lower income levels.

In addition, a much larger percentage of nonwhites tend to be renters than is true for the San Francisco population as a whole. Seventy-five percent of San Francisco's nonwhite households were renters in 1960 compared with only 65 percent for the population as a whole. Only 78 percent of all households with incomes below $5000 rented, while 87 percent of nonwhite households in the same income category were renters. Thus in the short run nonwhites would be more adversely affected than whites because a larger share are renters. (See Figures XV and XVI.)

Further, within any given income class nonwhite households tend to consume less housing than white households. Figures XIII and XIV illustrate that nonwhite renters at each income level pay less rent, on the average, than do white renters. Because nonwhite households consume less housing, they also pay lower property taxes than white households. Hence, any percentage reduction in property taxes would reduce the property tax bill of white households in a given income class more than the tax bill of nonwhite households. At the same time nonwhite households would be affected in the same way as white households by the income or earnings tax. Table XXI indicates the resulting long-run net effect on nonwhite renters and contrasts it with the net effect on all renters. Over the range of income classes, the tax change would be $4 to $7 more favorable for renters as a group than for nonwhite renters. Thus in both the short run and the long run nonwhites would benefit less than whites from potential reductions in rents and property taxes.

FIGURE XI

DISTRIBUTION OF RENTERS IN SAN FRANCISCO
BY INCOME CLASS

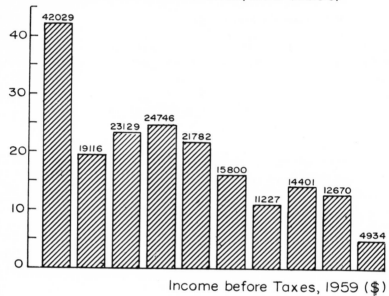

Number of Renters in San Francisco, 1960 (OOO's)

Income before Taxes, 1959 ($)

FIGURE XII

DISTRIBUTION OF HOMEOWNERS IN SAN FRANCISCO
BY INCOME CLASS

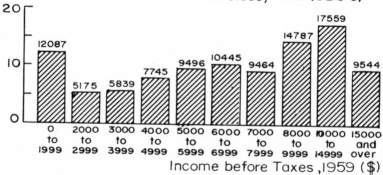

Number of Homeowners in San Francisco, 1960 (OOO's)

Income before Taxes, 1959 ($)

Source: U.S. Bureau of the Census, *1960 Census of Housing: Metropolitan Housing*, Vol. II, pp. 159-46 and 159-47.

FIGURE XIII

ESTIMATED MEDIAN MONTHLY RENT PAID
BY EACH INCOME CLASS, FOR ALL RENTERS
AND FOR NONWHITE RENTERS, 1960

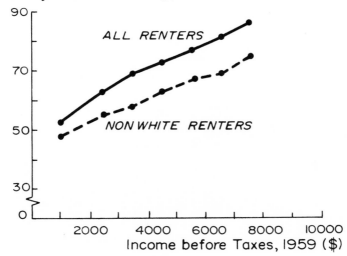

FIGURE XIV

ESTIMATED MEDIAN VALUE OF HOME OWNED
FOR EACH INCOME CLASS, FOR ALL HOMEOWNERS
AND FOR NONWHITE HOMEOWNERS, 1960

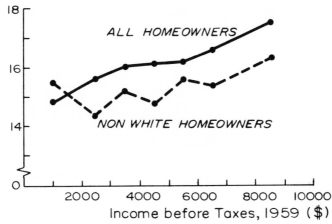

Source: U.S. Bureau of the Census, *1960 Census of
Housing: Metropolitan Housing,* Vol. II, pp. 159-46,
159-47, 159-56 and 159-57.

FIGURE XV

DISTRIBUTION OF NONWHITE RENTERS IN SAN FRANCISCO BY INCOME CLASS

Number of Nonwhite Renters in San Francisco, 1960

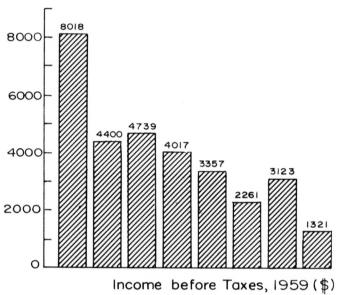

Income before Taxes, 1959 ($)

FIGURE XVI

DISTRIBUTION OF NONWHITE HOMEOWNERS IN SAN FRANCISCO BY INCOME CLASS

Number of Nonwhite Homeowners in San Francisco, 1960

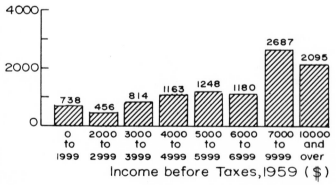

Income before Taxes, 1959 ($)

Source: U.S. Bureau of the Census, *1960 Census of Housing: Metropolitan Housing,* Vol. II, pp. 159-56 and 159-57.

TABLE XXI

A COMPARISON OF THE NET BURDEN ON ALL SAN FRANCISCO RENTERS WITH THAT
ON NONWHITE RENTERS OF A ONE PERCENT LEVY ON ALL PERSONAL INCOME EARNED
IN SAN FRANCISCO, ALL UNEARNED INCOME OF SAN FRANCISCO RESIDENTS,
AND ALL BUSINESS INCOME, 1967-68

Money income before taxes	Income tax payment	Average property tax payment		Property tax savings		Savings after federal tax deductions	
(1)	(2)	(3)	(4)	(5)	(6)	(7)	(8)
		All S.F.	Non-white	All S.F.	Non-white	All S.F.[a]	Non-white[a]
$ 2,064	$ 7	$103	$ 84	$22	$18	$ 15 (12)	$ 11 (9)
3,354	22	130	109	29	24	6 (6)	2 (2)
4,902	40	144	124	31	27	-7 (-7)	-11 (-10)
6,450	57	163	139	36	31	-17 (-17)	-21 (-21)
7,804	73	164	141	36	31	-30 (-30)	-34 (-34)
9,675	94	178	153	39	34	-43 (-44)	-47 (-48)
12,642	124	190	152	42	34	-64 (-66)	-70 (-72)
17,415	168	215	172	47	38	-91 (-97)	-98 (-104)
35,217	352	196	157	43	34	-185 (-232)	-191 (-244)

[a]The figures in parentheses result when it is assumed that all landlords
for all income classes are subject to a federal marginal tax rate of 20
percent.

Source: See Tables XIV and XX.

CONCLUSIONS: DECREASING REGRESSIVITY IN THE LOCAL TAX STRUCTURE

As previously stated, this chapter has inquired into
the ways that a movement toward local income taxes would
affect the equity of a local tax system. Eleven types of
local income taxes were examined to determine their
effect on the total local tax bill of San Francisco residents. This examination supports the claim that the
property taxes presently paid by San Francisco residents
are highly regressive. Property tax payments by renters
ranged from 3.9 percent of income before taxes for those
having incomes of $3400 to 0.6 percent for those having
incomes of $35,000. For homeowners, property taxes
varied from 9.8 percent to 2.7 percent of income.

In contrast, even flat-rate income taxes are
slightly progressive. (This results from the exclusion
of certain types of income.) Thus using local income tax

revenues to reduce property tax rates might lessen the regressivity of the local tax system. Table XXII, which presents the results for one of the taxes, indicates that this is in fact the case. Taxes on renters, previously ranging from 3.9 to 0.6 percent of money income before taxes, would now range from 3.7 to 1.1 percent. The change is the consequence of the enactment of the local income tax, the subsequent fall in property tax rates, and the long-run adjustment in the housing industry.

Simultaneously the effective rates on homeowners would fall from a range of 9.8 to 2.7 percent to a range of 8.5 to 2.9 percent. For homeowners and renters combined, the long-run effective rates would fall from a range of 5.1 to 2.0 percent to one of 4.8 to 2.3 percent. For both homeowners and renters local tax bills as a percent of money income would rise in the long run for those with high incomes, while they would fall for those with low incomes. In both the long run and the short run the regressivity of the tax structure would be slightly reduced. The progressivity-regressivity index (PRI) for renters and homeowners combined falls from 1.46 to 1.37 in the short run, and from 1.46 to 1.23 in the long run.[17]

An even stronger progressive influence on the tax structure would be exerted if a supplement to the state personal income tax were enacted. This too can be seen in Table XXII. For homeowners and renters combined, the before-tax-change rates range from 5.1 to 2.0 percent. The after-tax-change rates range from 4.6 to 3.6 percent. However, the 50 percent supplement to the California personal income tax raises less than the other local income levies considered. In addition it would be likely to have adverse effects on the location decisions of high-income households if levied solely by one community: To be effective in raising sizable amounts of revenue a tax of this type must be enacted on a regional or statewide basis.

TABLE XXII

LOCAL PROPERTY TAXES AS A PERCENT OF INCOME BEFORE TAX CHANGE;
AND LOCAL PROPERTY TAXES PLUS LOCAL INCOME TAXES AS A
PERCENT OF INCOME AFTER THE TAX CHANGE[a]

Before Tax Change

Money income before taxes	Taxes		Taxes as percent of money income before taxes		
	Homeowners	Renters	Homeowners	Renters	Combined[b]
(1)	(2)	(3)	(4)	(5)	(6)
$ 3,354	$328	$130	9.8	3.9	5.1
4,902	292	144	6.0	3.0	3.5
6,450	364	163	5.6	2.6	3.3
7,804	393	164	5.0	2.1	3.0
9,675	453	178	4.7	1.8	3.0
12,642	485	190	3.8	1.5	2.7
17,415	607	215	3.5	1.2	2.5
35,217	944	196	2.7	0.6	2.0

After Tax Change

Money income before taxes	Taxes			Taxes as percent of money income before taxes				
	Homeowners	Renters		Homeowners	Renters		Combined[b]	
(1)	(2)	(3)	(4)	(5)	(6)	(7)	(8)	(9)
		Short run	Long run		Short run	Long run	Short run	Long run
Type VII								
$ 3,354	$286	$152	$124	8.5	4.5	3.7	5.4	4.8
4,902	272	184	151	5.5	3.8	3.1	4.1	3.6
6,450	345	220	180	5.3	3.4	2.8	3.9	3.4
7,804	382	237	194	4.9	3.0	2.5	3.6	3.3
9,675	449	272	221	4.6	2.8	2.3	3.6	3.3
12,642	499	314	254	3.9	2.5	2.0	3.2	3.0
17,415	633	383	309	3.6	2.2	1.8	3.1	2.9
35,217	1,031	548	381	2.9	1.6	1.1	2.5	2.3
Type X								
$ 3,354	$295	$130	$117	8.8	3.9	3.5	4.9	4.6
4,902	263	144	130	5.4	2.9	2.7	3.4	3.2
6,450	327	164	146	5.1	2.5	2.3	3.1	2.9
7,804	365	176	158	4.7	2.3	2.0	3.0	2.8
9,675	445	222	196	4.6	2.3	2.0	3.2	3.1
12,642	510	280	242	4.0	2.2	1.9	3.1	3.0
17,415	699	410	342	4.0	2.4	2.0	3.3	3.2
35,217	1,500	1,337	866	4.3	3.8	2.5	4.1	3.6

[a]The types of local income tax employed in these calculations are a one percent levy on all earned and unearned income of residents, all earned income of nonresidents, all business income, with no exemptions or deductions (Type VII), and a 50 percent supplement to the California personal income tax (Type X). The short-run tax payment of renters after the tax changes is simply the sum of the income tax and the before-tax-change property tax.

[b]Calculated by multiplying the number of renters in each income class by the average tax in that class, doing the same for homeowners, then adding the products together. The total tax figure is then divided by the total number of households in each income class.

Sources: See Tables XIII, XIV, XVI and XX.

CONCLUSION

These examples indicate that the use of local income tax revenues to reduce pressure on property taxes would lessen the regressivity of the local tax system. The evidence further shows that the rates at which local income levies are usually set assure that the reduction in regressivity is small. Many policymakers may consider that the progressive influence of flat-rate taxes fails to offset the problems connected with any new tax. In their minds much higher tax rates would be needed to make the adoption of an income tax worthwhile. In this case, the tax would have to be enacted on an areawide basis if adverse effects on location decisions are to be minimized.

Policymakers must also note that the use of income tax revenues to reduce property tax revenues will have a particularly adverse effect on renters in both the long and short run. Renters would be faced with an additional income tax, but would have little reason to expect lower rents in the short run. As low-income groups and non-white households are primarily composed of renters, these groups would be especially adversely affected by the new tax. Policymakers should give careful consideration to this fact.

Two other factors may increase or decrease the slight progressive influence of local income taxes. First, business would pay lower total local taxes if income tax revenues were used to reduce property tax rates. Depending upon how business distributes this benefit, it might either enhance or offset the progressivity resulting from local income taxes. Second, capitalization of lower property taxes would lead to an increase in the value of property. To the extent that property, both residential and business, is concentrated in the hands of the higher income classes, the progressive influence of the tax would be lessened. These two matters are dealt with in the following chapters.

NOTES TO CHAPTER IV

1. See G. Alden Sears, "Incidence Profiles of a
Real Estate Tax and an Earned Income Tax: A Study in the
Formal Differential Incidence of Selected Local Taxes,"
National Tax Journal, 17(4): 340-356 (1964); and Melvin
and Ann White, "A Personal Income Tax for New York City:
Equity and Economic Effects" in New York University
Graduate School of Public Administration, *Financing
Government in New York City* (New York: 1966), pp. 449-
491. See also Ursula Hicks, "The Terminology of Tax
Analysis," *Economic Journal*, 56(221): 38-50 (1946). Mrs.
Hicks defines "formal" incidence as "the social account-
ing calculation of the proportion of people's incomes
paid over to taxing authorities in a defined period."
P. 49.

2. These conclusions are arrived at in a static
framework, through partial analysis. This chapter
stresses that it is necessary to consider the period of
adjustment to a new tax as movement from one equilibrium
point to the next. But partial equilibrium analysis is
just that--partial. If the results of partial analysis
are not clear cut, general equilibrium analysis may lead
to reversals in conclusions.

3. The limited amount of empirical evidence available supports the assumption that local income taxes are
used in lieu of higher property taxes. Elizabeth Doran
found that: "While income taxes usually have been introduced under conditions of severe financial stress, with
the primary objective the capture of additional revenue,
the evidence suggests that in practice the income tax
has to some degree acted as a substitutive rather than
supplemental source of revenue, and in particular has
taken some of the pressure off the property tax." See
"Tax Structure in Cities Using the Income Tax," *National
Tax Journal*, 21(2): 147-152 (1968), p. 152. A study

prepared by the Ohio Municipal League showed that 67 Ohio cities with local income taxes had property tax rates which were substantially below the property tax rates of 120 Ohio cities that had no local income tax. The property tax rate for the income tax cities averaged $6.08 per $1000 of assessed value while the rate of the non-income tax cities was $12.94. See Ohio Municipal League, Ch. I note 5. Adapted from Table IV, "State Totals For Property and Income Tax Rates, Collections, and Valuations," n.p.

4. For an illuminating discussion concerning the legality of income taxation by local governments in California, see Donatas Januta, "The Municipal Revenue Crisis: California Problems and Possibilities," 56 *California Law Review* 6: 1525-1558 (1968). See esp. pp. 1540-1558. Januta concludes that the municipal income tax should be no less an exclusively municipal affair for charter cities (San Francisco is a charter city) than is the occupational license tax. Therefore, at least for the present, the imposition of such a tax by charter cities would not be expected to be in conflict with the California State Constitution.

5. Pennsylvania, Department of Internal Affairs, *The Local Tax Enabling Act of 1965* (Harrisburg: 1966).

6. See Robert A. Sigafoos, Ch. I note 14, p. 79.

7. In Michigan these agreements are imposed by a state uniformity statute that prescribes a rate of one percent for residents, one-half percent for nonresidents. A resident is allowed credit for taxes paid to another city as a nonresident. In the case of Maumee and Toledo, Ohio, each city retains only 50 percent of the tax collected from the nonresident labor force. Throughout Ohio the *situs* of employment takes precedence over the place of residence. Though it is not legally required, cities generally allow their residents credit for income taxes paid to other local units. In other cases the surrounding cities have not retaliated. And in Missouri

only the central cities have been authorized by the State
Legislature to levy the local earnings tax.

8. In the case of Baltimore, the local tax is a
fixed percentage of the state income tax and thus automatically includes the deductions and exemptions allowed
in the state tax base.

9. In New York City, corporate profits are taxed at
5.5 percent while 2.0 percent is the highest rate levied
on any other form of income.

10. Melvin and Ann White calculated the coefficients
of variation of two types of income taxes and of existing
property taxes in the City of New York. See Melvin and
Ann White, Ch. IV note 1, p. 463. George F. Break, in a
report submitted to the State of California Advisory
Commission on Tax Reform in 1968, examined the horizontal
inequity of property taxes in California when viewed on
a benefits received basis. See *Agenda for Local Tax
Reform* (Berkeley: Institute of Governmental Studies,
University of California, 1970). Further evidence concerning the horizontal equity of the property tax on a
benefits received basis may be found in: U.S., Department of Commerce, Bureau of the Census, *1967 Census of
Governments, Taxable Property Values* (Washington, D.C.:
1968). This publication lists the coefficient of disper-
sion from the median assessment ratio for single-family
houses in all major cities in the United States in 1966.

11. Leo Grebler, "The Housing Problem: I. The Current Situation: The Housing Inventory: Analytic Concepts and Quantitative Change," *American Economic Review*,
41(2): 555-568 (1951); Chester Rapkin, Louis Winnick and
David M. Blank, *Housing Market Analysis* (Washington,
D.C.: U.S. Housing and Home Finance Agency, 1953);
David M. Blank and Louis Winnick, "The Structure of the
Housing Market," *Quarterly Journal of Economics*, 67(2):
181-208 (1953).

12. In March 1969 the Federal Housing Administration
published data indicating that on October 1, 1968, 0.9

percent of all typically owner-occupied units in San
Francisco were vacant, as were 4.2 percent of all typically renter-occupied units. On September 19, 1969, the
Federal Housing Authority released the results of a
postal vacancy survey conducted June 9-20, 1969: 0.9
percent of all "residences" were vacant, and 2.4 percent
of all "apartments" in San Francisco were vacant. (The
Post Office does not distinguish between owner-occupied
and renter-occupied.) A "residence" represents one possible stop with one possible delivery on a carrier's
route, and an "apartment" represents one possible stop
with more than one possible delivery. The above data
support the claim that San Francisco has a relatively
high occupancy rate.

13.   See Ralph Turvey, Ch. III note 10, loc. cit.

14.   Ernest M. Fisher and R.M. Fisher, *Urban Real
Estate* (New York: Henry Holt and Co., 1954). The Fishers
state that "Change in construction costs and new units
tends to lag behind changes in prices and rents. Costs
rise only after the rate of utilization has remained
above the critical zone for some time." P. 220.

15.   Ernest M. Fisher, *Urban Real Estate Markets:
Characteristics and Financing* (New York: National Bureau
of Economic Research, 1951), pp. 98-99.

16.   Richard F. Muth, "The Demand for Non-Farm
Housing" in *The Demand for Durable Goods* edited by
Arnold G. Harberger (Chicago: University of Chicago,
1960). Pp. 29-96, see especially p. 76.

17.   PRI equals the mean effective tax rate of individuals below the median income divided by the mean
effective tax rate of individuals above the median
income. See J.J. Launie, "Sales Tax Progressivity"
(June 1964), an unpublished paper cited by Harold Somers
in *The Sales Tax* (Sacramento: California Legislature,
1964), pp. 37-38.

APPENDICES
TO CHAPTER IV

Appendix A

CALCULATIONS FOR TABLE XII

Assumptions used in calculations:

1. Total employment increased as rapidly as did employment in those areas covered by unemployment insurance.

2. The ratio of workers living in San Francisco to the city's population has remained unchanged since 1960. The ratio of workers living *and* working in San Francisco to its population has also remained unchanged.

3. The ratio of all workers living in San Francisco to workers living in the city but working outside it has remained unchanged since 1960.

Population estimates are made by the California Department of Finance.

The method used in estimating total employment in San Francisco is as follows:

$$
\begin{array}{c}
\text{Total} \\
\text{employment} \\
\text{in S.F.,} \\
1967
\end{array}
=
\frac{
\begin{array}{c}
\text{Average number of} \\
\text{employees receiving} \\
\text{UI insured wages in} \\
\text{S.F. in 1967}
\end{array}
}{
\begin{array}{c}
\text{Average number of} \\
\text{employees receiving} \\
\text{UI insured wages in} \\
\text{S.F. in 1960}
\end{array}
}
\text{ X }
\begin{array}{c}
\text{Total employment} \\
\text{in S.F. in 1960}
\end{array}
;
$$

$$
\frac{353,399}{337,049} \text{ X } 421,490 = 441,974.
$$

The data on employees receiving UI insured wages are found in California Department of Employment *Report No. 127*. The *1960 Census of Population and Housing*, Table P-3 gives the total employment in San Francisco in 1960.

The following method is used to estimate the number living *and* working in San Francisco in 1967:

$$\begin{array}{l}\text{Number living} \\ \text{and working in} \\ \text{S.F. in 1967}\end{array} = \frac{\begin{array}{c}\text{S.F. population} \\ \text{in 1967}\end{array}}{\begin{array}{c}\text{S.F. population} \\ \text{in 1960}\end{array}} \times \begin{array}{l}\text{Number living} \\ \text{and working in} \\ \text{S.F. in 1960}\end{array} ;$$

$$\frac{747,500}{740,316} \times 313,219 = 316,038.$$

There is reason to be cautious when estimating the number of commuters working in San Francisco. The California Department of Employment in 1960 estimated the total number employed in San Francisco to be 473,500, compared to the Bureau of Census figure of 421,490. Using the more complete Census Bureau data, the 1967 estimate of total employment in San Francisco is 441,974, whereas the 1966 figure of the Department of Employment is 505,000. It is thus possible that commuters in 1967 numbered as many as 50,000 more than the estimate used in this study. Arthur D. Little, Inc. estimated 106,000 commuters in their 1967 *San Francisco Tax Study*.

Appendix B

COMMUTERS INTO AND OUT OF THE 43 LARGEST AMERICAN CITIES IN 1960

City	(a) Total employment in the city*	(b) Number working in city who also live in city*	(c) Number living in city who are employed*	(d)=(a)-(b) Number of commuters into the city*	(e) Rank	(f)=(d)/(a) Commuters as a percent of total city employment	(g) Rank	(h)=(c)-(b)[b] Number working outside city but living within*	(i)=(h)/(d) Out-commuters as percent of in-commuters	(j) Rank
New York City[a]	3435.9	3077.9	3234.1	358.0	2	10.4	42	156.1	43.6	14
Chicago	1687.9	1361.0	1470.2	326.9	3	19.4	32	109.2	33.4	24
Los Angeles	1190.3	780.9	1001.5	409.4	1	34.4	11	220.6	53.9	7
Philadelphia[a]	914.7	713.9	777.7	200.8	6	22.0	29	63.8	31.8	27
Detroit[a]	723.2	488.8	597.4	234.4	4	32.4	16	108.6	46.3	11
Baltimore[a]	413.1	309.2	355.6	103.8	11	25.1	26	46.4	44.6	13
Cleveland[a]	480.8	302.5	330.7	178.3	8	37.1	8	28.2	15.8	41
Houston	381.0	334.3	356.5	46.7	29	12.2	41	22.1	47.4	10
Milwaukee	343.3	266.3	295.8	76.9	19	22.4	28	29.4	38.3	18
San Francisco	421.5	313.2	336.6	108.3	10	25.7	24	23.4	21.6	38
St. Louis[a]	426.8	261.5	286.8	165.3	9	38.7	6	25.3	15.3	42
Boston	433.3	234.2	288.0	199.1	7	46.0	2	53.8	27.0	35
New Orleans	239.4	207.9	220.9	32.5	35	13.6	38	13.1	40.2	16
Washington, D.C.[a]	516.1	298.4	344.8	217.7	5	42.2	3	46.4	21.3	39
Dallas	317.8	264.4	281.5	53.5	26	16.8	36	17.1	32.0	25
Pittsburgh[a]	285.8	190.7	216.6	95.1	14	33.3	15	25.9	27.2	32
Atlanta	267.7	176.9	195.1	90.8	15	33.9	13	18.2	20.1	40
Minneapolis	277.8	181.4	205.7	96.4	13	34.7	10	24.3	25.2	36
Newark	183.0	97.7	301.7	85.4	17	46.6	1	204.0	239.0	2
Denver	242.2	176.5	197.4	65.7	24	27.1	20	20.9	31.8	27
Kansas City[a]	252.4	167.3	194.5	85.1	18	33.7	14	27.2	32.0	26
Phoenix	157.7	134.9	156.4	22.9	41	14.5	38	21.5	94.2	4
Cincinnati[a]	249.2	161.5	185.2	87.7	16	35.2	9	23.8	27.1	33
Seattle	281.1	207.5	228.2	73.6	22	26.2	22	20.7	28.1	30
Indianapolis	225.5	174.7	189.5	50.8	27	22.5	27	14.9	29.3	29
Buffalo	258.7	159.0	193.1	99.7	12	38.5	7	34.1	34.2	23
San Diego	292.7	217.9	238.1	74.8	21	25.6	25	20.2	27.0	34
Memphis	198.8	172.3	183.1	26.5	38	13.3	40	10.8	40.8	15
Fort Worth	151.3	124.0	138.7	27.2	37	18.0	34	14.6	53.7	8

Oklahoma City	148.4	118.3	128.8	30.1	36	20.3	30	10.6	35.1	21
Portland	195.4	132.2	145.9	63.3	25	32.4	17	13.7	21.7	37
Long Beach	146.1	100.5	144.7	45.6	30	31.2	18	44.3	97.1	3
Oakland	165.9	98.5	142.7	67.4	23	40.6	4	44.3	65.6	5
Rochester	194.8	119.3	126.0	75.5	20	38.8	5	6.7	8.8	43
San Antonio	166.5	160.8	193.9	5.7	43	3.4	43	33.1	582.1	1
Norfolk	142.4	115.9	125.1	24.4	40	17.2	35	9.1	37.4	19
Omaha	129.9	109.6	119.6	20.4	42	15.7	37	10.1	49.4	9
Columbus [a]	200.1	162.4	179.5	37.7	34	18.8	33	17.0	45.1	12
Dayton [a]	146.5	86.3	100.4	50.3	28	34.3	12	14.2	28.1	31
Toledo [a]	125.9	100.3	116.4	25.6	39	20.3	31	16.0	62.6	6
Louisville [a]	167.9	124.4	139.4	43.6	31	25.9	23	15.0	34.5	22
St. Paul	146.4	105.9	122.1	40.5	32	27.6	19	16.1	39.8	17
Birmingham	146.9	107.2	121.7	39.7	33	27.0	21	14.5	36.4	20

[a] Cities employing some form of local income tax in 1969.

[b] Cities facing possible retaliatory actions by surrounding communities must consider not only the number of in-commuters, but also the number of out-commuters--those living in the city and working outside--before imposing any form of local income taxation. See column (h).

Cincinnati reported that 38 percent of its income tax revenues were derived from nonresidents in 1964. See Cincinnati Income Tax Bureau, Report of 1964, *Cincinnati Income Tax Collections by Location* (February 1966), p. 2. Detroit, with a tax rate levied on earned income of nonresidents equal to half the rate levied on the earned income of residents, collected about 18 percent of income tax revenues from the nonresidents. See Tax Foundation, Inc., *City Income Taxes* (New York: 1967), p. 38. J.C. Phillips estimated that around 20 percent of Philadelphia's income tax revenues is collected from nonresidents. See his "Philadelphia's Income Tax After Twenty Years," *National Tax Journal*, 11: 241-253 (September 1958).

* Thousands.

Source: U.S. Bureau of the Census, *Census of Population and Housing, 1960*, Table P-3.

Appendix C

CALCULATIONS FOR TABLE XIII

Methods and sources used in estimating taxable income:

a and b: Both earned and unearned income of San Francisco residents are estimated from state personal income tax returns for San Francisco as reported by the California Franchise Tax Board in its 1966 *Annual Report*. Earned income is composed of wages and salaries and net proprietorship and partnership income. Unearned income includes interest, dividends, net rents and royalties and net capital gains.

Earned income of S.F. residents, 1967 =
Earned income of S.F. residents, 1965 X (1.09).

Unearned income of S.F. residents, 1967 =
Unearned income of S.F. residents, 1965 X (1.09).

The growth rate of adjusted gross income in San Francisco from 1960 to 1965 appears to be approximately 4½ percent per annum.

c: Earned income of in-commuters. The *1960 Census of Population and Housing* estimates the number of commuters from each suburb working in San Francisco. The increase in San Francisco commuters from 1960 to 1965 was apportioned so that the percentage of commuters from each suburb remained the same. Table P-3 of the *Census of Population and Housing* also gives the total number of employed males and females living in each suburb. If 75 percent of the total number are males, then it is assumed that 75 percent of the commuters from this particular suburb are male, 25 percent are female. (Intuitively it seems that males might be more apt to commute, but

because of lack of evidence the above has been assumed.)
Part 6 of the *1960 Population...Characteristics* gives the
median earnings of the males and females for each suburb
in 1960 (Table 76, p. 6-346).

California Department of Employment data indicate
that the average wage of those under UI insured employment increased by 25 percent from 1960 to 1966. It has
been assumed that an additional 4 percent increase occurred from 1966 to 1967.

For example, the earned income of commuters living
in Berkeley was calculated as follows:

$$\frac{\text{Male workers living in Berkeley, 1960}}{\text{Total workers living in Berkeley, 1960}} \times \begin{array}{c}\text{S.F. commuters}\\ \text{living in}\\ \text{Berkeley, 1967}\end{array} \times \begin{array}{c}\text{Median male}\\ \text{earned income}\\ \text{in Berkeley,}\\ \text{1960}\end{array} \times$$

$$1.25 \times 1.04 = \begin{array}{l}\text{Earned income of males}\\ \text{living in Berkeley and}\\ \text{working in S.F., 1967}\end{array}$$

PLUS

$$\frac{\text{Female workers living in Berkeley, 1960}}{\text{Total workers living in Berkeley, 1960}} \times \begin{array}{c}\text{S.F. commuters}\\ \text{living in}\\ \text{Berkeley, 1967}\end{array} \times \begin{array}{c}\text{Median female}\\ \text{earned income}\\ \text{in Berkeley,}\\ \text{1960}\end{array} \times$$

$$1.25 \times 1.04 = \begin{array}{l}\text{Earned income of females}\\ \text{living in Berkeley and}\\ \text{working in S.F., 1967}\end{array}$$

equals total earned income of people living in Berkeley
and working in San Francisco. The writer accepts the
possibility that earned income of commuters is generally
higher than that of noncommuters in a given suburban

area, but for lack of knowledge of a proper method to adjust for this, no adjustment has been made. As the data now stand, the average of commuter earnings in San Francisco is somewhat in excess of $7500.

d: Net corporate income in San Francisco must be estimated from state net corporate income. It was assumed that the ratio of San Francisco's corporate income to California's corporate income is the same as the ratio of San Francisco's UI insured payrolls to California's UI insured payrolls:

$$\text{Net corporate income in S.F., 1965} = \frac{\text{S.F. UI insured payrolls, 1965}}{\text{State UI insured payrolls, 1965}} \times \text{California net corporate income, 1965}$$

$$\$426{,}501{,}587 = \frac{2{,}409{,}000{,}000}{28{,}946{,}000{,}000} \times 5{,}126{,}221{,}000$$

San Francisco UI insured payrolls increased 21.4 percent from 1962 to 1966, about 4 percent a year. State UI insured payrolls increased 31.9 percent from 1962 to 1966, about 5 percent a year. California net corporate income increased about 37.9 percent from 1961 to 1965, about 6 percent a year. Influenced by these general trends, the author has assumed that San Francisco corporate income rose by 8 percent from 1965 to 1967.

$$1.08 \times 426{,}501{,}582 = 460{,}622{,}000.$$

e: Other business income includes that of proprietors and partners. Net proprietorship and partnership income increased 4.84 percent from 1960 to 1965, less than 0.8 percent a year. The Franchise Tax Board *Annual Report* indicates that proprietorship and partnership income in San Francisco in 1965 totaled $226,181,478. Hence for 1967 noncorporate business income is estimated to equal:

$$1.016 \times 226{,}181{,}478 = 229{,}000{,}000.$$

f: Earned income of out-commuters. In San Francisco in 1965 earned income composed 0.8038 of all adjusted gross income reported. Therefore,

$$\begin{array}{c}\text{Earned}\\\text{income of}\\\text{out-commuters}\end{array} = 0.8038 \ \text{X} \ \frac{\begin{array}{c}\text{Number of}\\\text{out-commuters,}\\ 1967\end{array}}{\begin{array}{c}\text{Number of}\\\text{workers living}\\\text{in S.F., 1967}\end{array}} \ \text{X} \ \begin{array}{c}\text{Total earned}\\\text{plus unearned}\\\text{income of S.F.}\\\text{residents, 1967}\end{array}$$

$$\$145,000,000 = 0.8038 \ \text{X} \ \frac{23,591}{339,629} \ \text{X} \ 2,575,000,000$$

g: Value of $600 exemptions. *Statistics of Income: State and Metropolitan Area Data for Individual Income Tax Returns*, Table 7, page 71 gives the value of exemptions taken in 1959 and 1961 in the San Francisco-Oakland SMSA. The number of $600 exemptions taken in 1959 and 1961 were 2,638,466 and 2,893,345, respectively. It has been assumed that 1960 exemptions were midway between 1959 and 1961, i.e., 2,765,905, which is equal to 99.4 percent of San Francisco-Oakland SMSA population in 1960. From this it was assumed that the number of exemptions taken in the area that commutes to San Francisco tends, in general, to equal the population. 1967 exemptions in San Francisco are assumed to be 747,500. To determine the number of exemptions per commuter in each county, total 1960 population of each of five counties--Alameda, Contra Costa, San Mateo, Marin and Solano--were divided by the number of workers living in each county in 1960.

Appendix D

PART I - CALCULATIONS FOR TABLE XIV

Re: Column 1, "Money income before taxes"

Income classes are taken from Bureau of Labor Statistics Survey of Consumer Expenditures, Report No. 237-37, *Consumer Expenditures and Income, 1960-61, Urban Places in the Western Region* (May 1964). The figures representing income classes are the average money income before taxes for each of the income classes set up by the Bureau of Labor Statistics. Each income class is raised 25 percent according to wage increases in San Francisco from 1960 to 1966. 1966 income is raised another 4 percent to get the 1967 income classes. BLS Report No. 237 also gives the average property tax paid by each of the income groups in urban places in the Western Region in 1960.

"Money income before taxes" includes the year's total money income from wages and salaries (including tips and bonuses) for all family members after deductions for such occupational expenses as tools, special required equipment, union dues; net income from self employment; and income from other earnings such as net rents, interest, dividends, Social Security benefits, pensions, disability insurance, trust funds, small gifts of cash, regular contributions for support, public assistance and other government payments. The value of two non-money items--food and housing received as pay--were counted as money income.

Re: Column 2, "Property tax payment"

1960 *Metropolitan Housing* (U.S. Census of Housing) data for the San Francisco-Oakland SMSA indicate that the value of the house of the homeowner having the median income of all San Francisco families owning and occupying their single-family dwelling was $17,300. The income of

this homeowner was about $7500. The tables assume that
the median income of all such homeowners has increased
by 25 percent between 1960 and 1966 to $9375 and by an
additional 4 percent to $9675 by 1967. What will be the
"average value" of the home owned by this median-income
family in 1966 and 1967? FHA data show the median value
of existing homes on which they have insured mortgages
to have increased from $13,043 in 1960 to $15,128 in
1965, an increase of 16 percent (*Statistical Abstract of
the U.S., 1966*, p. 747). This study assumes the average
value of the home owned by the median-income family in
San Francisco to equal (1.16 + .32/5)17,300 or $21,175
in 1967. Applying a median assessment ratio of 10.8
percent to single-family homes in San Francisco in 1966,
the assessed value would equal .108 x 20622. A tax rate
of $10.62 per $100 gives a property tax of $236.28.
For 1967, an assessment ratio of 24.4 percent is used
(*Controller's Annual Report of Assessed Valuation and
Tax Rates of the Counties of California* for fiscal year
1967-68) giving an assessed value of .244 x 21175 or
$5167 and a tax of .088 x 5167 or $454.70.

To estimate the property tax paid by other income
groups in 1966 and 1967 in San Francisco the following
calculation was made:

$$\begin{array}{c}
\text{Property tax} \\
\text{of income class} \\
\text{in S.F., 1966-67} \\
\text{(1967-68)}
\end{array}
=
\begin{array}{c}
\text{1960 property} \\
\text{tax of income} \\
\text{class (BLS} \\
\text{Report No. 237)}
\end{array}
\times
\dfrac{
\begin{array}{c}
\text{Property tax of} \\
\text{median-income} \\
\text{homeowner in S.F.,} \\
\text{1966-67 (1967-68)}
\end{array}
}{
\begin{array}{c}
\text{Property tax of} \\
\text{median-income} \\
\text{homeowner in urban} \\
\text{places in the} \\
\text{Western Region, 1960} \\
\text{(Report No. 237-37)}
\end{array}
}$$

Taking the income class of $2064 in 1967-1968 as an
example:

$$\$302.55 = \$129.34 \times \dfrac{454.70}{193.90}.$$

PART II - CALCULATIONS FOR TABLE XV

Re: Column 2, "Average annual rent"

The average rent paid in 1960 by each income class is obtained from BLS Report No. 237-37. These figures are then each inflated by 16.2 percent--the increase in San Francisco rents according to *The Consumer Price Index: U.S. City Average and Selected Areas*. It was assumed that the rent paid equaled 9.5 percent of the value of the rented property. The assessment ratio (.244) was then multiplied by the estimated value of the rented property. Finally, in order to get the property taxes paid, the estimated assessed value was multiplied by the tax rate (.088). It was assumed that 20 percent of the tax falls on the site and is borne by the land-lord, while the remaining 80 percent falls on the renter.

Appendix E

THE EFFECTIVE RATE OF A 50 PERCENT SURTAX LEVIED ON THE STATE
INCOME TAX IN SAN FRANCISCO IN 1967

Money income before taxes[a]	AGI[b]	Average deductions[c]	Average size of credit[d]	(Tax assessed -credit) x .50[e]	S.F. adjust-ment[f]	g= (f)/(a)
$ 2,064	$ 764	$ 639	31	0	0	0.0
3,354	2,205	771	35	0	0	0.0
4,902	4,000	1,040	46	0	0	0.0
6,450	5,755	1,201	50	1	1	0.0
7,804	7,253	1,711	56	8	12	0.2
9,675	9,357	1,785	60	29	44	0.5
12,642	12,352	2,153	64	67	90	0.7
17,415	16,814	2,691	64	151	195	1.1
35,217	34,817	4,592	64	790	1,141	3.2

[a]See Appendix D, Part I.

[b]AGI is money income before taxes minus Social Security and public unemployment benefits, private pensions and retirements, public social assistance and private relief, and military allotments and pensions. Derived from U.S. Bureau of Labor Statistics *Report No. 237* (see notes to Appendix D), and adjusted for 1967.

[c]The average deductions for each AGI class were obtained by dividing the total amount of deductions in the state in that class by the total number of tax returns in that class.

[d]The following steps were taken to estimate the average amount of credit for each income class: The average value of exemptions for each income class was obtained by dividing the number of returns in the class into the total value of exemptions for that class. Up to $3000, exemptions were assumed to be $1500 or a fraction thereof; above $3000 the exemptions were assumed to be $600. Example: For a given income class, assume exemptions averaged $3500. The average credit is estimated as follows: 3000/1500 ($25) + 500/600 = $56.67 ≃ $57.

[e]1967 state income tax rates are applied to AGI minus deductions and the credits are then subtracted. This is then multiplied by .50.

[f]For any given AGI class the tax assessed per return was lower for the state than for San Francisco. For the AGI class concerned, the ratios (R) of San Francisco tax per return to California tax per return were: 1.61, 1.57, 1.52, 1.35, 1.29, and 1.47. (f) = (R) x (e).

Appendix F

THE EFFECT OF IMPUTED RENTALS

When the imputed rental of their own homes--minus interest, insurance and upkeep expenses--is added to the income of homeowners, the ratio of property tax to income is significantly reduced for homeowners.

Money income before taxes	Property taxes as a percent of money income before taxes[a]	Property tax as a percent of money income before taxes[a] when net imputed rent is included in income[b]
$ 2,064	14.7	11.8
3,354	9.8	8.3
4,902	6.0	5.5
6,450	5.6	5.3
7,804	5.0	4.8
9,675	4.7	4.5
12,642	3.8	3.7
17,415	3.5	3.4
35,217	2.7	2.6

[a]For homeowners in San Francisco in 1967.

[b]Imputed rent is assumed to equal 7.5 percent of the value of owned homes. Mortgage interest, property insurance, repair and replacement expenses, property taxes and other expenses must be subtracted from the imputed rent to find the net addition to income. These expenses are obtained from BLS Report No. 237-37 for urban areas in the West, 1960-1961. 1960-1961 expenses are increased 22.4 percent to arrive at 1967 figures, the same as the estimated increase in home values.

The Spenders' Welfare Effect

INTRODUCTION

The business community, as noted in Chapter III, has
generally benefited from the adoption of local taxes on
business and personal income. This benefit rests on the
large share of property taxes paid by the business community in all major U.S. cities--a share that would pre-
sumably be reduced by the imposition of a local income
tax. Table XXIII presents the revenues that would be
raised by each type of local income tax considered in
this study; the property tax savings that would accrue to
business if all income tax revenues were used to replace
an equal amount of property tax revenues; the income tax
payment made by business; and the change in total local
tax payments made by business. We see that under each
type of local income tax considered the business community would pay substantially lower local taxes.

This lower tax bill may ultimately accrue to the
benefit of business, wage-earner or consumer groups. Due
to competition, businesses may pass the benefits of lower
taxes on to consumers in the form of lower prices or they
may raise wage and salary payments. The likelihood of
this outcome is increased by the pressure for higher
wages and salaries that withholding of local income tax
payments generates. Finally, as after-tax profits
increase, returns to invested capital may also increase,
thus passing the tax reduction on to owners of capital.
In practice, some combination of all three outcomes seems
likely, with consumers, wage earners and businesses each
benefiting to some extent.

TABLE XXIII

THE EFFECT OF DIFFERENT TYPES OF MUNICIPAL INCOME TAXES ON
TOTAL LOCAL BUSINESS TAXES IN SAN FRANCISCO IN 1967

(1) Type of local income tax	(2) Local income tax revenues	(3)[a] Business property tax savings	(4) Business income tax payment	(5) Local tax savings for business
	(thousands)	(thousands)	(thousands)	(thousands)
I	$34,870	$18,132	$ -	$18,132
II	29,820	15,506	-	15,506
III	28,370	14,752	-	14,752
IV	25,750	13,390	-	13,390
V	20,690	10,759	-	10,759
VI	39,490	20,528	4,606	15,922
VII	41,780	21,713	6,896	14,817
VIII	48,710	25,318	13,813	11,505
IX	55,580	28,905	20,688	8,217
X	23,000	11,960	-	11,960
XI	36,720	19,094	6,896	12,198

[a](3) = .52(2)

Source: See Table XIII.

The sum of these outcomes is known as the "spenders'
welfare effect." Formally, this is defined as the effect
that price changes will have on the real income of individuals, whether through a change in wages and returns
to capital or through a change in the price of goods and
services. The replacement of property taxes by local
income taxes will clearly generate such an effect. The
precise nature of this effect, i.e., the distribution of
benefits among consumers, wage earners and business, will
increase or decrease the slight progressive influence of
local income taxes noted in the previous chapter.

PREVIOUS STUDIES OF THE SPENDERS' WELFARE EFFECT

Previous studies of municipal income taxes have
given inadequate attention to the spenders' welfare
effect. J.R. Fahey's examination of municipal income
taxes in Boston contains no attempt to ascertain the
effect's significance.[1] G.A. Sears simply assumes that
any change in local property taxes paid by business would
affect only the residents of the community; he considers
only the case in which 100 percent of the tax is shifted
forward to consumers.[2] This type of assumption becomes
useless when considering a tax change under which considerable tax exporting is certain to occur, with the total
price reduction benefits not limited to residents alone.

The Whites, in their examination of the municipal
income tax proposed for New York City, did make assumptions permitting estimates of the spenders' welfare
effect.[3] They assume that 25 percent of the business
property tax rests on land, and 20 percent on wages and
property income. Thirty percent is shifted forward to
resident consumers, 50 percent to nonresident consumers.
Only the distribution of the 30 percent shifted forward
to resident consumers is considered in the Whites' estimate of tax burdens according to income class.

The present study is concerned primarily with the
effect of lower local business tax bills on the residents
of San Francisco. How much will San Francisco residents

benefit from the forward and backward shifting of this change in taxes? Estimation of this effect, though difficult, is extremely important if we are to ascertain the total result of a municipal income tax on the real income of different income classes in San Francisco.

ESTIMATION PROCEDURES

Several types of information and several assumptions are required in order to estimate the size of the spenders' welfare effect.

Division of Property Taxes and Income Taxes According to Type of Business

The property tax bill paid by each type of business and the probable income tax bill must first be ascertained. The data available permitted a rough breakdown of net local tax reductions according to type of business: commercial, industrial, or state-assessed utility, transportation and communication enterprises. The methods and data used to arrive at the estimates are discussed in Appendix A for this chapter.

Assumptions Needed to Divide the Effect Between Residents and Nonresidents

Three assumptions must be made in order to divide the spenders' welfare effect between residents and nonresidents. First, the tax reduction must be allocated between that portion passed on to consumers and that portion passed back on to wages, salaries and capital. The second, the portion passed backward, must be divided between that borne by wages and salaries and that borne by capital. Third, ownership of capital must be allocated between residents and nonresidents.

Rather than limit the analysis to one set of assumptions that cannot be supported without qualification,

several cases are examined. One extreme case assumes
that the entire tax reduction is passed forward to consumers. The opposite extreme is also considered, i.e.,
the entire tax reduction is passed back on to wages,
salaries and capital. The case in which half the tax
reduction is passed forward, half passed back, is also
discussed. Similarly, three distributions of the share
of the tax reduction that is passed backward are
examined: (a) the case in which 100 percent of the tax
reduction passed backward falls on wages and salaries;
(b) the case in which 100 percent falls on capital; and
(c) the case in which 50 percent falls on wages and
salaries while the other 50 percent falls on capital.

Unfortunately, few empirical studies have attempted
to estimate the shares of local capital owned by residents and nonresidents.[4] As a result, in order to divide
between residents and nonresidents the backward-passed
taxes falling on capital, we have assumed that from 10
to 50 percent of all business property in San Francisco
is owned by residents. These two percentages are
employed as limits in the following estimates. They
appear reasonable in light of the city's narrow geograph-
ical confines and the number of nationally owned corporations within its borders.

For each form of local income taxation examined,
the various combinations of assumptions result in 11
separate estimates of the spenders' welfare effect.
These combinations of assumptions are illustrated graphi-
cally in Figure XVII.

Tax Reductions Passed on to Consumers: The Division Between Residents and Nonresidents

Given the above information, the purchases made
from each type of business must be divided between residents and nonresidents in order to allocate the tax
reductions passed forward. Estimates indicate that 41
percent of all forward-shifted tax changes accruing to
commercial enterprises would ultimately benefit residents

120

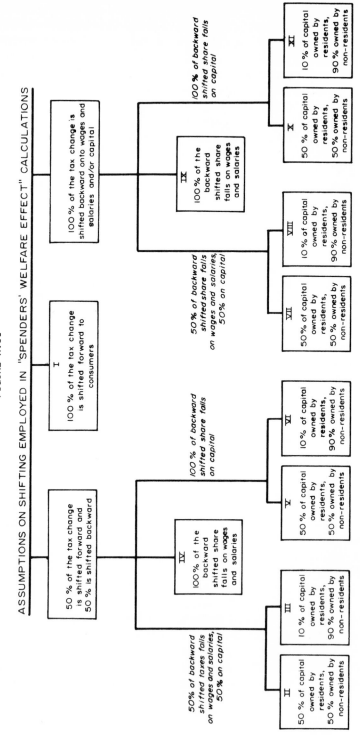

FIGURE XVII

ASSUMPTIONS ON SHIFTING EMPLOYED IN "SPENDERS' WELFARE EFFECT" CALCULATIONS

of San Francisco. For public utility-transportation-communications enterprises and for industrial enterprises the figures are 65 and 21 percent, respectively. The methods used to arrive at these estimates are presented in Appendix A for this chapter.

Tax Reductions Passed on to Wages and Salaries: The Division Between Residents and Nonresidents

Only part of the tax change passed backward on to wages and salaries would affect residents. Thus some estimate of the amount of taxes falling on the wages and salaries of residents and nonresidents was needed. U.S. census data, combined with California Department of Employment figures, indicate that 67 percent of all employees in the commercial sector are residents of San Francisco. This suggests that 67 percent of a tax reduction passed on to wages and salaries in the commercial sector would benefit residents. The same sources indicate that 70 percent of all public utility, transportation, and communication sector workers are residents, while the Chamber of Commerce *Industrial Survey* estimates that 62 percent of all industrial workers are residents.[5]

The Division of the Spenders' Welfare Effect Among Income Classes

Finally, in order to determine the spenders' welfare effect for each income class it was necessary to divide the total effect first among classes, then among the families in each class. The method and data used for this purpose are discussed in Appendix A for this chapter.

THE INFLUENCE OF THE SPENDERS' WELFARE EFFECT ON
THE DISTRIBUTION OF INCOME UNDER A VARIETY OF ASSUMPTIONS

Figure XVII represents the 11 sets of assumptions upon which estimates of the spenders' welfare effect were

based. For example, set II assumes that (a) 50 percent
of the tax change is shifted forward onto purchasers,
and 50 percent is shifted backward onto owners of factors
of production; (b) 50 percent of that shifted backward
falls on wages and salaries, 50 percent on capital; and
(c) 50 percent of the capital is owned by residents, 50
percent by nonresidents. On the other hand, set XI
assumes that (a) 100 percent is shifted backward; (b)
100 percent of that shifted backward falls on capital;
and (c) 10 percent of capital is owned by residents.
Thus, the magnitude of the spenders' welfare effect
experienced by residents depends heavily on the set of
assumptions employed in the estimates.

Table XXIV presents estimates of the spenders' welfare effect for one type of local income tax: a one percent tax on the earned and unearned income of San Francisco residents; the income earned in San Francisco by
nonresidents; and all business income. Columns (2)
through (12) present the estimates of the spenders' welfare effect under each of the 11 sets of assumptions.
Under assumption set II, the third column of Table XXIV,
it can be seen that benefits due to the spenders' welfare
effect range from $5 for the lowest income class to $87
for the highest income class. These benefits are gained
in the form of higher wages or salaries, higher dividends
or lower prices. Under assumption set XI, the last
column, it can be seen that benefits range from $0 to
$34. The spenders' welfare effect benefits are much
smaller in this case because it is assumed that 100 percent of the lower taxes is passed backward on to wages,
salaries and capital; that 100 percent of the benefit
accrues to capital; and that 90 percent of capital is
owned by nonresidents. This means that residents receive
only 10 percent of the benefit from lower business taxes.
Further, under assumption set II the benefits accruing
to residents are more evenly distributed among income
classes than under assumption set XI. In the latter case
benefits accrue only to owners of capital, who are much
less evenly distributed among income classes than are
either wages and salaries or consumption expenditures

TABLE XXIV

DISTRIBUTION OF THE SPENDERS' WELFARE EFFECT FOR EACH INCOME CLASS UNDER VARIOUS ASSUMPTIONS

Spenders' Welfare Effect under a Type VII Tax[a] (in dollars)

(1) Money income before taxes	(2) I	(3) II	(4) III	(5) IV	(6) V	(7) VI	(8) VII	(9) VIII	(10) IX	(11) X	(12) XI
					Various shifting assumptions						
$ 2,064	$ 8	$ 5	$ 4	$ 6	$ 4	$ 3	$ 3	$ 2	$ 5	$ 1	$ 0
3,354	10	8	7	10	5	4	8	7	13	2	0
4,902	15	11	10	15	6	5	11	10	20	2	0
6,450	17	15	14	21	9	8	15	14	27	2	0
7,804	28	18	17	26	10	9	18	17	34	3	1
9,675	25	22	21	31	12	10	23	22	48	6	1
12,642	30	30	29	42	18	12	30	28	55	18	4
17,415	37	40	37	53	27	20	43	34	69		
35,217	55	87	53	60	114	45	119	50	66	172	34

[a]Type VII tax: A 1 percent tax on both earned and unearned income of San Francisco residents; on income earned in San Francisco by nonresidents; and on all business income.

Tables XXV and XXVI of this chapter show the effect
of the tax change--for one type of local income tax--
when the spenders' welfare effect is included. For
example, with a Type VII income tax the effect of the
tax change on the after-tax income for homeowners ranged
from +$59 to -$87 with the spenders' welfare effect
excluded. If the spenders' welfare effect under assumption set II is included, the effect of the tax change
ranged from +$64 to $0.[6] Similar figures for Type I and
Type IX taxes are contained in Appendix B for this chapter.

CONCLUSIONS

Examination of Tables XXIV, XXV and XXVI clearly
indicates that assumptions have a significant influence
on the distribution of the spenders' welfare effect. For
example, the larger the share of the tax change exported,
the smaller is the effect on residents of the community.
Similarly, the greater the share of the tax change
accruing to capital, the greater the benefit to the
higher income classes. This, of course, is due to the
concentrated ownership of various forms of wealth in the
upper income classes. Conversely, if the entire tax
reduction is assumed to be passed forward, the spenders'
welfare effect is more evenly distributed than in any
other case. This too is predictable, for current consumption expenditures vary less among income classes
than do either wages and salaries or the ownership of
income-earning assets.

Two consequences of the spenders' welfare effect,
however, are relatively independent of the set of
assumptions employed. First, when the spenders' welfare
effect is included, it appears that homeowners as a group
may well benefit from the imposition of a local income
tax. Only a very small percentage of homeowners--those
with high incomes and relatively inexpensive housing--
would find their after-tax real income lower than prior
to the tax change. Conversely, the spenders' welfare
effect would be unlikely to offset the higher income

TABLE XXV

THE NET BURDEN ON SAN FRANCISCO RESIDENT-HOMEOWNERS OF A TYPE VII
LOCAL INCOME TAX WHEN THE INCOME TAX REVENUES ARE USED TO REDUCE PROPERTY
TAXES AND THE SPENDERS' WELFARE EFFECT IS INCLUDED

(1)	(2)	(3)	(4)	(5)	(6)	(7)	(8)	(9)	(10)	(11)	(12)	(13)
Money income before taxes	Type VII Tax Without spenders' welfare effect	Net savings after federal tax deductions under various shifting assumptions (see Figure XVII)										
		I	II	III	IV	V	VI	VII	VIII	IX	X	XI
$ 2,064	$ 59	$ 67	$ 64	$ 63	$ 65	$ 63	$ 62	$ 62	$ 61	$ 64	$ 60	$ 59
3,354	42	52	50	49	52	47	46	50	49	55	44	42
4,902	20	35	31	30	35	26	25	31	30	40	22	20
6,450	19	36	34	33	40	28	27	34	33	46	21	19
7,804	11	39	29	28	37	21	20	29	28	45	13	11
9,675	4	29	26	25	35	16	14	27	26	44	7	5
12,642	-14	16	16	15	28	4	2	16	14	41	-8	-13
17,415	-26	11	14	11	27	1	-6	17	8	43	-8	-22
35,217	-87	-32	0	-34	-27	+27	-42	+32	-37	-21	+85	-53

TABLE XXVI

THE NET BURDEN ON SAN FRANCISCO RESIDENT-RENTERS OF A TYPE VII
LOCAL INCOME TAX WHEN THE INCOME TAX REVENUES ARE USED TO REDUCE PROPERTY
TAXES AND THE SPENDERS' WELFARE EFFECT IS INCLUDED

(1)	(2)	(3)	(4)	(5)	(6)	(7)	(8)	(9)	(10)	(11)	(12)	(13)
	Type VII Tax	Net savings after federal tax deductions under various shifting assumptions (see Figure XVII)										
Money income before taxes	Without spenders' welfare effect	I	II	III	IV	V	VI	VII	VIII	IX	X	XI
$ 2,064	$ 13	$ 21	$ 18	$ 17	$ 19	$ 17	$ 16	$ 16	$ 15	$ 18	$ 14	$ 13
3,354	6	16	14	13	16	11	10	14	13	19	8	6
4,902	-7	8	4	3	8	-1	-2	4	3	13	-5	-7
6,450	-17	0	-2	-3	4	-8	-9	-2	-3	10	-15	-17
7,804	-30	-10	-12	-13	-4	-20	-21	-12	-13	4	-28	-30
9,675	-43	-18	-21	-22	-12	-31	-33	-20	-21	5	-40	-42
12,642	-64	-34	-34	-35	-22	-46	-52	-34	-36	-9	-58	-63
17,415	-94	-57	-54	-57	-41	-67	-74	-51	-60	-25	-76	-90
35,217	-185	-130	-98	-132	-125	-71	-140	-66	-135	-119	-13	-151

taxes faced by renters. Thus inclusion of this effect makes clearer the adverse effect on renters of a movement toward local income taxes.

Second, the inclusion of the spenders' welfare effect--under most sets of assumptions--lessens the progressive influence of the movement toward greater reliance on local income taxes. This can be seen in Table XXVII. Column (6) indicates that average tax rates ranged from 4.8 to 2.3 percent of money income before taxes prior to the inclusion of the spenders' welfare effect. When this is included, the average tax rates drop to 4.5 and 2.0 percent, respectively, indicating a slightly more regressive tax structure.[7]

One additional point must be emphasized. Though Table XXIV indicates that in each case the spenders' welfare effect increases the real income of all income classes, or leaves it unchanged, a particular household may not fare so well. As noted in Chapter III, not all businesses would benefit from the tax change: Some would be confronted with an increased local tax bill. Despite the overall spenders' welfare effect, their employees, customers and owners could experience lower wages, higher prices or lower returns to capital.

The spenders' welfare effect, then, may take many forms and have many consequences. In some cases the consequences will be far from negligible. Thus policymakers must take them into account along with the other effects of the local income tax.

TABLE XXVII

LOCAL PROPERTY TAXES AS A PERCENT OF INCOME BEFORE
TAX CHANGE; LOCAL PROPERTY TAXES + LOCAL INCOME TAXES[a]
AS A PERCENT OF INCOME AFTER THE TAX CHANGE; AND AFTER THE
TAX CHANGE WITH THE SPENDERS' WELFARE EFFECT INCLUDED

Before the tax change

(1) Money income before taxes	(2) Taxes Renters	(3) Taxes Homeowners	(4) Renters	(5) Homeowners	(6) Combined
$ 2,064	$103	$303	5.0	14.7	-
3,354	130	328	3.9	9.8	5.1
4,902	144	292	3.0	6.0	3.5
6,450	163	364	2.6	5.6	3.3
7,804	164	393	2.1	5.0	3.0
9,675	178	453	1.8	4.7	3.0
12,642	190	485	1.5	3.8	2.7
17,415	215	607	1.2	3.5	2.5
35,217	196	944	0.6	2.7	2.0

After the tax change

2,064	90	244	4.4	11.8	-
3,354	124	286	3.7	8.5	4.8
4,902	151	272	3.1	5.5	3.6
6,450	180	345	2.8	5.3	3.4
7,804	194	382	2.5	4.9	3.3
9,675	221	449	2.3	4.6	3.3
12,642	254	499	2.0	3.9	3.0
17,415	309	633	1.8	3.6	2.9
35,217	381	1,031	1.1	2.9	2.3

Spenders' welfare effect included[b]

2,064	85	239	4.1	11.6	-
3,354	116	278	3.5	8.3	4.5
4,902	140	261	2.8	5.3	3.4
6,450	165	330	2.6	5.1	3.2
7,804	176	364	2.2	4.7	3.0
9,675	199	427	2.0	4.4	3.0
12,642	224	469	1.8	3.7	2.7
17,415	269	593	1.5	3.4	2.6
35,217	294	944	0.8	2.7	2.0

[a]The type of local income tax employed in these calculations is a one percent levy on all earned and unearned income of residents, earned income of
nonresidents, and business income, with no exemptions or deductions.

[b]Assumptions for the spenders' welfare effect included: (1) 50 percent
of the tax change is shifted forward and 50 percent is passed backward; (2)
of that which is passed backward, 50 percent is passed on to wages and salaries and 50 percent is passed on to capital; (3) 50 percent of the capital
used in San Francisco businesses is owned by residents and 50 percent by
nonresidents. This is case II in the spenders' welfare effect estimates.

NOTES TO CHAPTER V

1.   J.R. Fahey, "The Advisability and Probable
Effects of a Local Income or Sales Tax in Boston"
(unpublished Ph.D. dissertation, Department of Economics,
Massachusetts Institute of Technology, 1967).

2.   See G. Alden Sears, Ch. IV note 1.

3.   See Melvin and Ann White, Ch. IV note 1, p. 473.

4.   Existing tax export studies have made a wide
range of assumptions.   One study, dealing with the incidence of local taxes in New York City, assumed that 50
percent of all property owners, both corporate and individual, live outside the city (Alan D. Donheiser, "The
Incidence of the New York City Tax System" in the New
York University Graduate School of Public Administration's *Financing Government in New York City* [New York:
1966], pp. 153-207).   This assumption was justified on
the basis that: "no reliable estimate of ownership of
business property has ever been made and, indeed, [it]
can never be made without an extensive sample of tax
returns from the entire nation." (P. 201.)

The few existing comprehensive studies dealing with
the incidence of state taxes have contained a variety of
assumptions.   O.H. Brownlee, in his study of Minnesota
taxes, assumed that taxes on both corporate and noncorporate business income and real property affected only
the income of residents ("Estimated Distribution of Minnesota Taxes and Public Expenditure Benefits," *Studies
in Economics and Business No. 21* [Minneapolis: University
of Minnesota Press, 1960], pp. 21 and 23).   Therefore,
residents of the state bore the entire burden or received
the entire benefit of a tax change affecting the rate of
return on capital in Minnesota.

In their study dealing with the incidence of taxes in Michigan, Musgrave and Daicoff assumed that Michigan residents would pay from 3.58 percent of all "cost taxes" falling on profits, and would pay from 3.58 percent to 100 percent of corporate profits taxes, depending on whether the company was "national" or "local" (R.A. Musgrave and Darwin Daicoff, "Who Pays Michigan Taxes?" in *Michigan Tax Study Staff Papers, 1958* [Lansing: 1958]. Pp. 131-183, see especially pp. 171-173).

Using a questionnaire to help determine capital ownership, the Wisconsin tax study found that two-thirds of all corporate business property in Wisconsin was owned by residents (University of Wisconsin Tax Impact Study Committee, *Wisconsin's State and Local Tax Burden* [Madison: 1959], p. 44). The Wisconsin study assumed all noncorporate business property to be owned by residents.

5. See Appendix A to this chapter for a more complete explanation.

6. Spenders' welfare effect calculations for types of local income taxes appear in Appendix B for this chapter.

7. Calculation of the progressivity-regressivity index (PRI) also indicates that the inclusion of the spenders' welfare effect lessens the progressive influence of a local income tax. The PRI equals the mean effective tax rate of individuals below the median income divided by the mean effective tax rate of individuals above the median income. For property taxes paid directly and indirectly by homeowners and renters prior to the tax change the PRIs were 2.84 and 2.46, respectively. Following the tax change, but without the spenders' welfare effect, the indexes became 1.94 and 2.07 for homeowners and renters, indicating a decrease in the regressivity of the tax burden. The inclusion of the spenders' welfare effect raises these indexes to 2.13 for both homeowners and renters.

Calculation of PRI, an example: (calculated from Table XXVII)

Renters				Homeowners			
5.0	1.8			14.7	4.7		
3.9	1.5	$\dfrac{14.5}{5.1}$	= 2.84	9.8	3.8	$\dfrac{36.1}{14.7}$	= 2.46
3.0	1.2			6.0	3.5		
2.6	.6			5.6	2.7		
14.5	5.1			36.1	14.7		

(See J.J. Launie, Ch. IV note 17.)

Appendix A

BASIC STEPS IN THE CALCULATION OF
THE SPENDERS' WELFARE EFFECT

Step 1: The reduction in the overall local tax bill
of business must be measured. The division of property
taxes between business and residential property was taken
from San Francisco Assessor's Office records for real
property. The personal property division of the assessor's office had no breakdown between commercial, industrial and state-assessed business enterprises. Because
of this, Table V on page 20 of the *San Francisco Tax
Study* was used to allocate personal property among the
various types of business. It was assumed that the share
of personal property owned by each business sector--
industrial, commercial and state-assessed--was the same
in 1967-1968 as in 1965-1966. Consequently the breakdown
of property taxes was assumed to be 48, 32, 8 and 12 percent for residential, commercial, industrial and state-
assessed property, respectively. Therefore 52 percent of
the property tax reduction that would occur because of
local income taxes would accrue to the benefit of business. Commercial property would receive 32 percent of
the tax reduction flowing to business; industrial property would receive 8 percent; and state-assessed communication, transportation and utility property would receive
12 percent. (See table, p. 133.)

Income taxes were allocated by the taxable income of
each type of business. For proprietorships and partner-
ships, the California Franchise Tax Board *Annual Report*
gives the income earned according to type of business in
1964. Corporate income for each type of business in San
Francisco was determined in the following manner:

$$\frac{\text{S.F. payroll of business}}{\text{State payroll of business}} \times \begin{array}{c}\text{California}\\\text{corporate income}\\\text{of this type}\\\text{of business}\end{array} = \begin{array}{c}\text{S.F.}\\\text{corporate}\\\text{income of}\\\text{this business}\end{array}$$

132

Assessed property values, 1967-68

Type of property	Real property	Personal property	Total	Percent
Residential	$1,133,437,223	$ -	$1,133,437,223	48
Commercial	548,838,329	191,884,000	740,722,329	32
Industrial	132,371,143	57,316,000	189,787,143	8
State-assessed	187,260,000	91,708,850	278,968,850	12
				100

Payroll data were obtained form the *County Business
Patterns, 1964* published by the U.S. Census Bureau. The
present study assumes that in San Francisco commercial
enterprises would pay 66.6 percent of any flat-rate
income tax on business, while industrial and state-
assessed enterprises would pay 14.5 and 18.9 percent,
respectively.

Step 2: Those benefits of tax reductions that are
passed forward and backward must be divided among the
various income classes in San Francisco. Bureau of Labor
Statistics (Supplement 3--Part A to Report No. 237-37,
July 1964) and *1960 Census of Housing: Metropolitan
Housing* (Vol. II, p. 159-47) data make it possible to
calculate the share of total spending by San Francisco
residents that is done by each income class. Multiplying
the average current consumption expenditures for each
class by the number in that class gives the total spending by San Francisco residents for current consumption.
Each income class is then allocated part of the tax
reduction passed forward according to its share of total
spending for current consumption. To get the average
spenders' welfare effect for each class, the total amount
for each income class is divided by the number of households in the class.

Step 3: Two methods were used to allocate the share
of the tax reduction passed forward between residents
and nonresidents. For the retail, wholesale, service,
finance and public utility sectors, a method developed
by Homer Hoyt was employed, with one modification, to
estimate the division of goods and services (produced
and/or sold in San Francisco) between those purchased by
residents and those purchased by nonresidents.[1] The Hoyt
method (a) divides the local labor force according to
type of employment; (b) determines the percentage of
national income earned by the city being analyzed; (c)
applies this percentage to the total number in the nation
engaged in each type of employment; and (d) subtracts
this number from local employment in the sector. The
final operation gives the number of workers producing
for nonresident purchasers. Because residents make many

purchases outside of the city the Hoyt method appears likely to overestimate the amount of production serving residents. Hence, the method used in this study estimates that the amount of employment in a city that serves residents equals the percent of national population in the city multiplied by the number nationally employed. As per capita income in San Francisco is above the national average, this method provides lower estimates than does the normal Hoyt method.

Using 1963 *Census of Business* data, the modified Hoyt method indicated that approximately 62, 34, 33 and 35 percent of the retail, wholesale, service and financial sectors, respectively, were employed in production for San Francisco residents.[2] Weighting each of these trades by total employment, approximately 41 percent of all commercial activity in San Francisco is due to residents, 59 percent to nonresidents. Similar estimation methods indicated that 65 percent of all employment in public utilities and public transportation and communication (c-t-u) enterprises provided for the needs of residents.[3]

An industrial survey made by the Greater San Francisco Chamber of Commerce was used to estimate the share of the industrial sector, excluding utilities, transportation and communications.[4] This survey indicated that only 21 percent of the output of local manufacturers is sold to buyers in San Francisco City and County. Therefore the present study assumed that 79 percent of any tax reduction passed forward by the industrial sector of the business community fell on nonresidents, 21 percent on residents.

The manufacturing and c-t-u sectors together comprise the industrial sector. Approximately 42 percent of their total production goes to residents. The figure is arrived at by weighting 65 percent and 21 percent by the local employment in the two sectors.

Step 4: To determine the share of the tax reduction that accrued to the wages and salaries of residents and the share that accrued to nonresidents, it was necessary

to determine what share of employment was nonresident in
each business sector. The 1960 U.S. *Census of Population, Characteristics of Population*, Vol. 1, part 6,
Table 75, and the California Department of Employment's
data in *California Community Labor Market Surveys, 1960-
61* were used to make these estimates. The former gave
the total number of San Francisco residents working in
each business sector in San Francisco. The latter gave
the total employment in each sector in San Francisco.
Including the trade, financial and service sectors under
the heading "commercial," it was found that 67 percent
of commercial employees in San Francisco are residents
of San Francisco. Seventy percent of the employees of
the c-t-u sector are residents. The *Industrial Survey,
1968* estimated that 58 percent of manufacturing employees
lived in San Francisco. Therefore it is assumed that in
the commercial sector 67 percent of the tax reductions
passed back to wages and salaries go to residents; in the
c-t-u sector 70 percent; in the manufacturing sector only
58 percent.

Step 5: The tax reductions that were passed back
on to capital had to be divided between residents and
nonresidents. To derive estimates a variety of assumptions about capital ownership were made. These are presented in Figure XVII.

Step 6: Once the share of the backward-passed tax
reduction that affected San Francisco residents was
determined, some method was needed to divide it among the
various income classes. The Internal Revenue Service's
Statistics of Income: Individual Returns, 1960 was used
for this purpose. The percentage of adjusted gross
income (income after exemptions and deductions) in the
form of wages, salaries and dividends was used to derive
the share of total before-tax income that each income
class received in the form of wages, salaries and dividends. These figures were then interpolated to estimate
the share of money income before taxes that would be
composed of wages, salaries and dividends in each of the
Bureau of Labor Statistics income classes. The average
figure for a member of each income class was multiplied

by the number in the income class to get the total of
wages, salaries and dividends received by residents of
San Francisco and the share going to each income class.
The share of the tax reduction falling on the wages and
salaries of residents was divided among income classes
according to their share of total wages and salaries.
The share of the tax reduction falling on capital owned
by residents was divided among income classes according
to their share of total dividends received.

NOTES TO APPENDIX A

1. Homer Hoyt and Arthur M. Weimer, "Economic Base Analysis" in *The Techniques of Urban Economic Analysis*, ed. R.W. Pfouts (West Trenton, New Jersey: Chandler-Davis, 1960). Pp. 20-38, see especially 26-31.

2. Sales Management's *Survey of Buying Power* estimated that the population of the United States was 190,020,500 at the end of 1963. The population estimated for San Francisco was 745,300, or .392 percent of the U.S. population. See Vol. 92, no. 12 (June 10, 1964), pp. 19, 252.

For those retail trades listed in the *1963 Census of Business*, 53,231 were employed in San Francisco. 0.392 percent of those employed in the United States equals 32,884 or only 62 percent of those actually employed. For wholesale trades listed in the *1963 Census of Business*, 35,452 were employed in San Francisco. Of the total employed in the U.S., 0.392 percent equals 12,077, 34 percent of those actually employed. Following the same procedure for services, 38,404 were actually employed, while, if the percent employed in San Francisco equaled the percent of total U.S. population in San Francisco, only 12,753 would have been employed. This is equal to only 33 percent of those actually employed. See Vol. 1, part 1, pp. 6-62; Vol. 5, pp. 6-24; Vol. 7, part 1, pp. 6-11.

Though the *Census of Business* does not cover all types of retail or wholesale trades or services, this study assumes that the percentages estimated here would hold if all businesses were included in the census.

For the finance, insurance and real estate sectors the figures were taken from the *1960 Census of Population*. 0.392 percent of total U.S. employment in these fields equaled 10,562 in 1960, or only 35 percent of total 1960 employment in these areas in the City and County of San Francisco.

3. Seven percent of total employment in the State of California in 1963 was in the areas of transportation, communications, gas, electricity and sanitation. It is assumed that the same percentage of total employment would be sufficient to serve the needs of San Francisco residents. Seven percent of total employment in San Francisco in 1963 equaled 33,551 which was 65 percent of the 51,800 actually employed.

4. Greater San Francisco Chamber of Commerce, *Industrial Survey* (April 1968). Studies of metropolitan New York; Cincinnati, Ohio; Denver, Colorado; Albuquerque, New Mexico; and Madison, Wisconsin indicated that 34, 9, 27, 15, and 17 percent, respectively, of all goods manufactured in these areas were consumed in the areas. The Regional Plan Association, Inc., *The Economic Status of the New York Metropolitan Region in 1944* (New York: 1944); Cincinnati City Planning Commission, *The Economy of the Cincinnati Metropolitan Area* (Cincinnati: 1946); Denver Planning Office, *Working Denver: An Economic Analysis* (Denver: 1953); Federal Reserve Bank of Kansas City and the University of New Mexico, *The Economy of Albuquerque, New Mexico, 1949* (Albuquerque: 1949); John W. Alexander, "The Basic-Nonbasic Concept of Urban Economic Functions," *Economic Geography*, 30(3): 246-261 (1954).

Appendix B

TYPE I AND TYPE IX LOCAL INCOME TAXES

TABLE A

DISTRIBUTION OF THE SPENDERS' WELFARE EFFECT FOR EACH INCOME CLASS UNDER VARIOUS ASSUMPTIONS

Spenders' Welfare Effect under a Type I Tax[a] (in dollars)

Money income before taxes	The various shifting assumptions (see Figure XVII)										
	I	II	III	IV	V	VI	VII	VIII	IX	X	XI
$ 2,064	$ 9	$ 6	$ 6	$ 8	$ 5	$ 5	$ 4	$ 3	$ 6	$ 1	$ 0
3,354	13	11	11	14	8	7	9	8	16	3	1
4,902	18	17	15	21	10	9	13	12	24	2	0
6,450	21	20	19	27	12	11	18	17	33	3	1
7,804	25	24	23	33	14	13	22	21	42	3	1
9,675	31	30	29	42	18	16	28	26	52	4	1
12,642	37	37	36	52	22	19	37	34	67	7	1
17,415	45	49	45	65	34	25	53	44	84	22	4
35,217	68	107	65	74	140	53	146	61	80	211	42

Spenders' Welfare Effect under a Type IX Tax[b] (in dollars)

Money income before taxes	I	II	III	IV	V	VI	VII	VIII	IX	X	XI
$ 2,064	$ 4	$ 3	$ 3	$ 3	$ 2	$ 2	$ 2	$ 1	$ 3	$ 1	$ 0
3,354	6	5	5	7	4	3	4	4	7	1	0
4,902	8	7	7	10	5	4	6	6	11	1	0
6,450	10	9	9	12	6	5	8	8	15	1	0
7,804	11	11	11	15	6	6	10	10	19	1	0
9,675	14	13	13	19	8	7	13	12	23	2	0
12,642	17	17	16	24	10	9	17	15	30	3	1
17,415	21	22	20	29	15	11	24	20	38	10	2
35,217	31	46	29	34	58	24	61	27	36	96	19

[a] Type I tax: A 1 percent tax on both earned and unearned income of San Francisco residents and on the income earned in San Francisco by nonresidents.

[b] Type IX tax: A Type I tax plus a 3 percent tax on all business income.

TABLE B

THE NET BURDEN ON SAN FRANCISCO RESIDENT-HOMEOWNERS OF LOCAL INCOME TAXES
OF TYPES I AND IX WHEN THE INCOME TAX REVENUES ARE USED TO REDUCE
PROPERTY TAXES AND THE SPENDERS' WELFARE EFFECT IS INCLUDED

Type I Tax

Money income before taxes	Without spenders' welfare effect	Net savings after federal tax deductions under various shifting assumptions (see Figure XVII)										
		I	II	III	IV	V	VI	VII	VIII	IX	X	XI
$ 2,064	$ 48	$ 57	$ 54	$ 54	$ 56	$ 53	$ 53	$ 52	$ 51	$ 54	$ 49	$ 48
3,354	32	45	43	43	46	40	39	41	40	48	35	33
4,902	11	29	28	26	32	21	20	24	23	35	13	11
6,450	7	28	27	26	34	19	18	25	24	40	10	8
7,804	-1	24	23	22	32	13	12	21	20	41	2	0
9,675	-9	22	21	20	33	9	7	19	17	43	-5	-8
12,642	-28	9	9	8	24	-6	-9	9	6	39	-21	-27
17,415	-44	1	5	1	21	-10	-19	9	0	40	-22	-40
35,217	-108	-40	-1	-43	-34	+32	-55	38	-47	-28	+103	-66

Type IX Tax

Money income before taxes	Without spenders' welfare effect	I	II	III	IV	V	VI	VII	VIII	IX	X	XI
$ 2,064	$ 81	$ 85	$ 84	$ 84	$ 84	$ 83	$ 83	$ 83	$ 82	$ 84	$ 82	$ 81
3,354	61	67	66	66	68	65	64	65	65	68	62	61
4,902	37	45	44	44	47	42	41	43	43	48	38	37
6,450	37	47	46	46	49	43	42	45	45	52	38	37
7,804	33	44	44	44	48	39	39	43	43	52	33	32
9,675	30	44	43	43	49	38	37	43	42	53	32	30
12,642	13	30	30	29	37	23	22	30	28	43	16	14
17,415	7	28	29	27	36	22	18	31	27	45	17	9
35,217	-46	-15	0	-17	-12	+12	-22	+15	-19	-10	+50	-27

TABLE C

THE NET BURDEN ON SAN FRANCISCO RESIDENT-RENTERS OF LOCAL INCOME TAXES
OF TYPES I AND IX WHEN THE INCOME TAX REVENUES ARE USED TO REDUCE
PROPERTY TAXES AND THE SPENDERS' WELFARE EFFECT IS INCLUDED

Type I Tax

Money income before taxes	Without spenders' welfare effect	Net savings after federal tax deductions under various shifting assumptions (see Figure XVII)										
		I	II	III	IV	V	VI	VII	VIII	IX	X	XI
$ 2,064	$ 12	$ 21	$ 18	$ 18	$ 20	$ 17	$ 17	$ 16	$ 15	$ 18	$ 13	$ 12
3,354	2	15	13	13	16	10	9	11	10	18	5	3
4,902	-12	6	4	3	8	-3	-4	1	0	12	-10	-12
6,450	-22	-1	-2	-3	5	-10	-11	-4	-5	11	-19	-21
7,804	-35	-10	-11	-12	-2	-21	-22	-13	-14	7	-32	-34
9,675	-49	-18	-19	-20	-7	-29	-31	-21	-23	3	-45	-48
12,642	-72	-35	-35	-36	-20	-50	-53	-35	-38	-5	-65	-71
17,415	-97	-52	-48	-52	-32	-63	-72	-44	-53	-13	-75	-93
35,217	-188	-120	-81	-123	-114	-48	-135	-42	-127	-108	+23	-146

Type IX Tax

Money income before taxes	Without spenders' welfare effect	I	II	III	IV	V	VI	VII	VIII	IX	X	XI
2,064	$ 23	$ 27	$ 26	$ 26	$ 26	$ 25	$ 25	$ 25	$ 24	$ 26	$ 24	$ 23
3,354	14	20	19	19	21	18	17	18	18	21	15	14
4,902	2	10	9	9	12	7	6	8	8	13	3	2
6,450	-8	2	1	1	4	-2	-3	0	0	7	-7	-8
7,804	-20	-9	-9	-9	-5	-14	-14	-10	-10	-1	-20	-21
9,675	-34	-20	-21	-21	-15	-26	-27	-21	-22	-11	-32	-34
12,642	-55	-38	-38	-39	-31	-45	-46	-38	-40	-25	-52	-54
17,415	-80	-59	-58	-60	-51	-65	-69	-56	-59	-42	-70	-78
35,217	-177	-146	-131	-148	-143	-119	-153	-116	-150	-141	-81	-158

Property Tax Capitalization

TAX CAPITALIZATION THEORY

The spenders' welfare effect discussed in the previous chapter illustrates the indirect effects the imposition of a local income tax may have on income distribution. When local income taxes are viewed as an alternative to higher property taxes, another indirect effect must be taken into account. This is tax capitalization: the process through which changes in property taxes are translated into changes in property values.

Capitalization may be defined as the process of computing the present value of a future string of payments. With regard to the property tax a popular textbook explains:

> It is generally argued that the tax will tend to capitalize, that is, to reduce, the selling price of the land by the capitalized sum of the tax. Thus if a parcel of land has been yielding an annual net income of $400, its selling price would have been roughly $8000, if 5 per cent is considered by investors to be the appropriate return on investments of this degree of risk and liquidity. But if a tax of $100 is imposed on the value of the land, the net yield will be cut to $300--under the assumption

> that no forward shifting is possible--
> the selling price will drop to $6000.[1]

This paragraph suggests that a rise in property taxes would decrease the wealth of real property owners. Conversely, a fall in property taxes would increase their wealth.

In many cases income tax revenues are viewed as an explicit means of altering or preserving the property tax structure--of maintaining or lowering current property tax rates. But the phenomenon of tax capitalization implies that by affecting property tax rates, income tax levies will also affect property values and the distribution of wealth. Clearly this aspect of local income taxes is one to which policymakers must devote attention. This chapter approaches the question by examining the actual effect of property tax changes on property values in the City and County of San Francisco.

EMPIRICAL EVIDENCE TO DATE

Few empirical studies of tax capitalization have been made, and the conclusions of those studies are not in complete agreement. One of the early attempts was made by Jens P. Jensen who, in his definitive work on property taxes, examined the prices of farmland in 13 states between 1919 and 1924. Jensen observed that although the market price of farmland fell significantly during this period, the net rent on farmlands, after taxes, remained 2.3 percent. "The capital value is the elastic element, being depressed by rising taxes and falling rents, so as to leave the net rent, clear of taxes, at 2.3 per cent for both years."[2] Jensen admits that he has not separated the effects of capitalization of taxes from other factors that caused land prices to decline from 1919 to 1924, but asserts that the evidence still points to fairly complete capitalization of property taxes on farmland.

In contrast, Daicoff's more recent study uses regression analysis to conclude that "all tests of the usually accepted capitalization doctrine produced results that were inconsistent with the doctrine."[3] Consequently claims that new owners should be subjected to additional taxes due to their capitalization of existing taxes are usually unjustified. Daicoff, it must be stressed, did not prove that property taxes are not capitalized. He demonstrated instead that the government expenditures made possible by the tax revenues may add more to the value of the property than the tax payments detract. That is, capitalization of expenditure benefits frequently offsets capitalization of the property tax. As a result new owners paid more for property than they would have if tax increases had not occurred.

Evidence of property tax capitalization has been found in two short studies completed since Daicoff's work. F.O. Woodard and R.W. Brady examined a sample of farmlands in Indiana and Ohio and found that the present value of the future income stream from property minus the present value of the future stream of tax payments on the property better explained the variance in sales prices than did the present value of the future income streams alone.[4] For these farmlands, higher taxes apparently were not accompanied by public expenditures that added as much to the future income stream as the taxes detracted.

In another study, Wicks, Little and Beck claim to "reinforce the conclusions of the Woodard-Brady investigation and give needed empirical reinforcement of the capitalization hypothesis."[5] Evaluating the effects of a reassessment in Missoula County, Montana, they collected data on actual sales prices and on taxes before and after the reassessment. The expected sale price was calculated by multiplying the assessed values by an average sale-to-assessment ratio derived from a sample of sales made prior to the reassessment. On the basis of these data the authors found that the larger the tax increase, the greater were the absolute decreases in expected sale prices--a conclusion lending support to the doctrine of tax capitalization. Wicks et al., however, implicitly assumed that expenditures were held constant despite the tax increase.

THE SAN FRANCISCO CASE

Recent property tax changes in San Francisco provide an opportunity for further assessment of the tax capitalization thesis. These changes were the result of the California Legislature's 1966 enactment of the Petris-Knox Bill (hereafter referred to as AB 80). AB 80 required that for each year

> through 1970-71, the assessor will assess all taxable property in his county at a uniform percentage of his estimate of full cash value. He may choose any ratio from 20 per cent to 25 per cent but must publicly announce the figure and apply the same percentage to all property regardless of its class. Beginning with the 1971-72 fiscal year, all locally assessable property will be assessed at 25 per cent of its value.[6]

In contrast, Arthur D. Little, Inc. estimated that prior to enactment of AB 80 assessment ratios for residential property in San Francisco were 10 percent for single-family units, 14 percent for dwellings with 2 to 4 units and 20 percent for those with 5 or more units.[7]

Because commercial and industrial properties in San Francisco were already assessed at between 20 and 25 percent of market value prior to passage of AB 80, San Francisco's reassessment shifted a larger share of the property tax bill onto residential property. By November 1967 residential property owners were faced with large increases in their property tax bills. Many owners of single-family dwellings found their property tax bills doubled.

This reassessment, with its resulting changes in property taxes, offers a unique opportunity to test the hypothesis of property tax capitalization. Seldom are tax bills changed by such large amounts within a short period, making more obvious any effect resulting from

the tax change. Even more important, there was no reason
to expect that the change in taxes on residential property would be accompanied by a change in government
expenditures benefiting this property. The result of
higher residential property taxes was expected to be, and
has been, lower taxes on business property rather than
increased expenditures benefiting property owners. Thus
this study of capitalization is not complicated by the
need to consider the consequences for property values of
increased government expenditures.

METHODOLOGY OF THE PRESENT STUDY

Time Periods and Samples

The full impact of AB 80 could not be expected to be
immediately evident in the San Francisco real estate market, for there are several points in time at which capitalization of a tax change may occur. The first is the
time when it becomes clear from political activities that
a tax change is forthcoming; second is the point at which
the forthcoming tax change is publicly announced; third
is the time when the homeowners and potential homeowners
learn the actual size of the change.

Thus in order to establish the point at which the
capitalization of the tax change occurred in San Francisco it was necessary to choose three separate samples
from the sample area.

AB 80 was signed into law on July 8, 1966 by Governor Edmund G. Brown. Therefore the first sample was
composed of sales made prior to the signing of AB 80--
between January 1, 1966 and July 8, 1966. Perhaps the
more astute homeowners could foresee the enactment of
AB 80 prior to this date. Nevertheless, July 8, 1966
seems the most appropriate date to begin an examination
of its impact, for after this date San Franciscans could
be fairly certain of a major change in residential
property taxes. Assessed values were about to increase
markedly; property tax burdens would rise.

A second sample was chosen from sales occurring
between September 1, 1966 and June 30, 1967. Between
November 1966 and June 1967, the assessor's office
reassessed residential property. The new values were
made public in the first week of July. Thus this period
followed the enactment of AB 80 but preceded notification
to homeowners of the new assessed value of their dwellings. Exact property tax bills, however, were not yet
established.

It would seem likely that a large amount of capitalization would occur between the two sample periods.
After AB 80's enactment, homeowners realized that homes
assessed at approximately 10 percent of full market value
would soon be assessed at 25 percent of full market
value. It was unlikely that tax rates would decrease
sufficiently to offset the higher assessments. Hence,
tax bills appeared certain to rise, but there was considerable uncertainty about the size of the increase.
In short, capitalization that occurred from Period I to
Period II took place without certain knowledge of the
size of the impending tax change.

The third sample was comprised of sales made between
September 15, 1967 and August 31, 1968 (see Table
XXVIII). On September 12, 1967 the tax rate applicable
to the new assessed values was made public; higher taxes
became a reality. Thus during this period the exact size
of the tax change was known to all homeowners. Data for
Sample III were collected to determine whether full capitalization had already occurred after reassessment or
whether further capitalization occurred after the
announcement of the new tax rate.

The area chosen for sampling lies mostly within the
Sunset District: bounded on the east and west by 10th
and 35th Avenues, respectively; bounded on the north and
south by Lincoln Way and Sloat Boulevard, respectively.
The area consists primarily of middle-income single-
family dwellings although there are some small apartment
buildings. The area was chosen as sufficiently homoge-
neous for sampling purchase on the basis of a street-by-
street examination of residential sections of San Francisco and talks with a realtor in the Sunset District.

TABLE XXVIII

SAMPLE INFORMATION FOR CAPITALIZATION STUDY

Sample number and period number	Time period in which sales occurred	Size of sample
I	January 1, 1966 to July 8, 1966	80
II	September 1, 1966 to June 30, 1967	131
III	September 15, 1967 to August 31, 1968	90

The data were collected in two ways. The first two samples were drawn through inspection of the Multiple Listing Service files of a large Sunset District realtor. To compile the third sample it proved easier to use the sales records that the San Francisco Assessor's Office maintained after July 1967.

Development of Price-Predicting Equations

Data collected for each piece of property in the three samples included sale price, the age of the property, the date of sale and assessed values for 1966 and 1967. The latter made possible calculation of the change in taxes (ΔT) between 1966 and 1967. But in order to examine the effects of the tax capitalization it was necessary to develop a model that would permit estimating what sale prices would have been had there been no tax increase.

In developing this model, data on Period I sales were used to estimate relationships that were then assumed to hold for Periods II and III. In testing for capitalization between Periods II and III, relationships existing in Period II were assumed to hold in Period III. In other words, it was assumed that without a tax change and an upward trend in housing prices, a home of a given age and assessed value should sell for the same price in Period II as in Period I.

Preliminary analysis of the data suggested two further points: (1) The selling price/assessed value ratios appeared to increase as selling price rose; and (2) the selling price/assessed value ratios appeared to rise as the age of the house increased. The two points are illustrated in Table XXIX. Together these observations suggested that for a given assessed value (S), selling price would increase with age (A). Therefore age was included in the price-predicting equation as well as assessed value. For the latter, 1967 rather than 1966 assessed values were chosen: In many cases the 1966 assessed value of residential properties had been established years earlier; thus the 1967 assessed values appeared to be better predictors of selling price whether the sale occurred in 1966 or 1967.

Though assessed value (S) appears more logically to be the dependent variable and selling price (P) the independent variable, P was regressed on S and A in order to develop the price-predicting equation. This resulted in *equation (1)* calculating the sales price in Period I.

$$P = 2370.13 + 4.804\ S + 44.957\ A$$
$$(2817.51)\quad (.407)\quad (32.819)$$

$$R^2 = .670$$

where P = selling price in Period I
 S = 1967 assessed value
 A = age of the dwelling
The figures in parentheses are standard deviations of the estimates.

The sale prices in the sample ranged from \$23,000 to \$46,000. The coefficient of S is significant at the .001 level, that of A at the .20 level. The regression has a

TABLE XXIX

VARIATIONS IN SALE PRICE TO ASSESSED VALUE RATIOS
ACCORDING TO SALE PRICE AND AGE

Property category	Sample size	Mean sale price to assessed value ratio	Standard deviation	Confidence level for difference in mean ratios
SAMPLE I				
Sale price				
below $25,000	12	5.068	.472	< 50 percent
$25,000-$29,999	33	5.409	.415	95 percent
$30,000-$34,999	42	5.639	.510	< 50 percent
$35,000 and over	13	5.668	.609	
Age[a]				
below 25 years	24	5.232	.374	90 percent
25 to 34 years	30	5.560	.509	negative
35 years and over	26	5.528	.451	
SAMPLE II				
Sale price				
below $25,000	18	4.804	.698	98 percent
$25,000-$29,999	71	5.231	.667	90 percent
$30,000-$34,999	52	5.465	.656	< 50 percent
$35,000 and over	10	5.578	1.083	
Age[a]				
below 25 years	18	4.929	.841	98 percent
25 to 34 years	63	5.210	.524	90 percent
35 years and over	50	5.391	.729	

[a]Of the 100 and 151 items originally selected for Samples I and II respectively, age data were available for only 80 items in Sample I and 131 items in Sample II. Items for which age data were not available were dropped from the samples.

standard error of only $2464, suggesting that the fit is reasonably good.

Since the age and 1967 assessed value of all parcels of property in Sample III are known, it is now possible to estimate what these properties would have sold for had there been no tax change, assuming that all other factors remained constant.[8] An adjustment must, of course, be made for rising prices. This was done by raising the prices predicted by *equation (1)* by the normal rise in real estate prices--2.6 percent annual rise for the period April 1966 to October 1968.[9]

Comparing these predicted prices with actual prices, it was then possible to estimate the effect of the tax change on the price of single-family dwellings using *equation (2)*. ΔP is the price at which the property actually sold less its predicted price. ΔT is the change in taxes: It was obtained by multiplying the 1966 and 1967 assessed values by the 1966 and 1967 tax rates, respectively, then subtracting the 1966 tax from the 1967 tax.

Evidence of Capitalization

The data presented in Table XXX demonstrate that capitalization of the property tax rise did occur between Periods I and III. The table is based on analysis of a sample of 90 single-family dwellings in the Sunset District, divided into three equal parts according to the size of the property tax increase. Only empirical results are presented here; those more interested in the statistical texts employed are referred to the Appendix.

Column (b) indicates that property taxes increased significantly from 1966 to 1967, following enactment of AB 80. This increase ranged from an average of $191 (for the third experiencing the lowest increase) up to an average of $289 (for the third experiencing the highest increase). Column (c) presents the difference between the actual sale price and the predicted sale

TABLE XXX

MEASUREMENT OF TAX CAPITALIZATION
OCCURRING BETWEEN PERIODS I AND III

(a) Third	(b) Average change in property taxes (ΔT)	(c) Average change in selling prices (ΔP)	(d) Difference in ΔP means	(e) Confidence level for difference in ΔP means	(f)[1] Capitalization ratio
1st	$191	$-2472	$ -607	< 50 percent	12.9
2nd	229	-3079	-1851	90 percent	13.4
3rd	289	-4930			17.1
				Average	14.5

Sample size = 90

The confidence level for the difference in ΔP means between the first and last thirds is 99 percent.

[1] (f) = - (c)/(b)

price of the property without the tax change: It indicates that these tax increases resulted in substantially
lower property values than would otherwise have been the
case. Property values for this sample of single-family
dwellings ranged from a decline of $2472 for that third
experiencing the smallest tax increases to a decline of
$4930 for that third experiencing the largest tax
increases. Columns (d) and (e) offer further evidence
that capitalization occurred--that larger tax increases
led to larger price effects.

Finally, column (f) presents the overall capitalization ratio--the ratio of the change in property tax to
the change in property value. In our sample, a $1 rise
in property taxes caused a $14.50 fall in property
values. This change may not, however, be entirely the
consequence of capitalization of tax changes resulting
from AB 80 between Periods I and III. It is, for
example, quite possible that the expectation of even
higher tax rates in the future has led to capitalization
of some of these higher rates in the period under consideration. Such expectations seem reasonable: San
Francisco's tax rate rose from $8.80 per $100 of assessed
value in 1967 to $10.23 in 1968, an increase of 16 per-
cent. If these expectations were capitalized, the estimated capitalization ratio will be higher than they would
be if only 1966-1967 changes were capitalized.

In contrast, if homeowners and purchasers believed
that the state or county would provide some kind of
relief to offset the effects of the reassessment on their
tax bills, the expected increase in future taxes would
be less, and property values would not fall by as much.
This influence would tend to lower the capitalization
ratio. The capitalization ratio would also be lowered
if some capitalization occurred prior to July 8, 1966,
the date on which AB 80 was signed into law.

Omitting these factors--whose influence is difficult to ascertain--from the analysis, the data presented
in Table XXX clearly support the theory of property tax
capitalization: A significant rise in residential

property taxes--unaccompanied by any significant increase in public services--caused the value of residential property to decline below its expected value. Further, the larger the tax increase, the greater the fall in property value.

The San Francisco data also indicate that a significant change in property taxes, combined with a relatively inelastic supply of single-family housing, may have a sizable impact on the net wealth of a large sector of a community. As the market value of their homes decreases, so too does their net wealth. In the case under study, the capitalization ratio indicates that the $200 tax increases faced by many homeowners were accompanied by $2600 to $3400 decreases in net wealth.

TAX CAPITALIZATION AND LOCAL INCOME TAXES

Tax capitalization does not invariably lead to decreased property values. When property taxes fall, property values and the net wealth of homeowners will increase.

It should be noted that renters will not experience this same increase in wealth. Further, lags in the housing market may mean that renters will not benefit in the short run from property tax reductions. It may take years before lower property taxes are fully passed on in the form of lower rents. Policymakers, when considering property tax changes, should examine which groups in the community are renters and which are property owners.

When property tax reductions are combined with the imposition of a local income tax, the overall redistribution effects become complex. The progressive effects of the income tax may be reduced or negated by capitalization of lowered property taxes. This will be especially true when ownership of property is concentrated in the hands of upper income groups. Thus the policymaker should investigate the impact of tax capitalization when considering changes in property taxes, alone or in conjunction with the imposition of a local income tax.

It is possible, of course, that increases or decreases in property taxes may be offset by changes in government expenditures. Thus the results of the study presented in this chapter in no way contradict findings that rising property taxes, which would by themselves tend to lower property values, are frequently accompanied by governmental expenditures that actually cause the market value of the property to increase.

NOTES TO CHAPTER VI

1.   John F. Due, *Government Finance*, 3d. ed.
(Homewood, Ill.: R.D. Irwin, 1963), pp. 365-366.

2.   Jens P. Jensen, *Property Taxation in the United
States* (Chicago: University of Chicago Press, 1931),
p. 73.

3.   Darwin W. Daicoff, "Capitalization of the
Property Tax" (unpublished Ph.D. dissertation, Department
of Economics, University of Michigan, 1961), p. 112.

4.   See "Inductive Evidence on Tax Capitalization,"
National Tax Journal, 18(2): 193-201 (1965).

5.   John H. Wicks, Robert A. Little, and Ralph A.
Beck, "A Note on Capitalization of Property Tax Changes,"
National Tax Journal, 21(3): 263-265 (1968).

6.   See California, *Statutes...*, 1966 First Extra-
ordinary Session, Chapter 147, Sec. 34, p. 658.

7.   Arthur D. Little, Inc., *San Francisco Tax Study,
1967, Report to Finance Committee, Board of Supervisors,
City and County of San Francisco*, p. 37.

8.   Readers interested in examining the tax capitalization that occurred between Periods I and II and Periods II and III are referred to the Appendix for this
chapter.

9.   Rather than using San Francisco data to determine the normal increase in real estate prices, the
average increase for the surrounding Bay Area (East Bay,
North Bay, Peninsula) during the period April 1966 to
October 1968 was used. The average annual rise for the
surrounding Bay Area for the period April 1966 to April

1967 was 1.6 percent; from April 1966 to October 1968, it was 2.6 percent annually. This method is more likely to reflect the changes in credit and other factors in the Bay Area housing market that occurred during the period of capitalization. However, it should be noted that from 1961 to 1966 the San Francisco price index for single-family dwellings averaged a 5.9 percent annual increase, while the increase for the surrounding Bay Area averaged only 4.4 percent. From 1964 to 1966 the annual rises in San Francisco and the surrounding area were 5.4 and 3.7 percent, respectively. Northern California Real Estate Research Committee, *Northern California Real Estate Report*, Fourth Quarter, 1968.

Appendix to Chapter VI

TAX CAPITALIZATION MODEL AND TESTS

This appendix provides a more detailed look at the tax capitalization results presented in Chapter VI. It presents a simple tax capitalization model; examines capitalization occurring from 1966 to 1967 and from 1967 to 1968; and employs additional statistical tests of capitalization, as well as a dummy variable approach.

A Tax Capitalization Model

The following model illustrates how capitalization of property taxes affects property values.

P = capitalized value of a property prior to an unexpected tax rate change (or reassessment).

A_j = value of services provided by property in year j, net of anticipated taxes prior to the tax change (or reassessment). For rental property A_j would represent the income stream net of anticipated taxes prior to the tax change.

P_t = capitalized value of a property after the unexpected tax rate change (or reassessment).

ΔT_j = anticipated change in the property tax bill for year j following the tax rate change (or reassessment), either positive or negative.

ΔP = capitalized value of the change in property taxes.

i = appropriate return to an investment of this particular degree of risk and liquidity (assumed constant for simplification).

(a) $\quad P = \dfrac{A_1}{(1+i)} + \dfrac{A_2}{(1+i)^2} + \ldots + \dfrac{A_n}{(1+i)^n} = \sum\limits_{j=1}^{n} \dfrac{A_j}{(1+i)^j}$

(b) $\quad P_t = \dfrac{A_1 - \Delta T_1}{(1+i)} + \dfrac{A_2 - \Delta T_2}{(1+i)^2} + \ldots + \dfrac{A_n - \Delta T_n}{(1+i)^n} =$

$$\sum\limits_{j=1}^{n} \dfrac{A_j - \Delta T_j}{(1+i)^j}$$

(c) $\quad \Delta P = P - P_t = \sum\limits_{j=1}^{n} \dfrac{A_j}{(1+i)^j} - \sum\limits_{j=1}^{n} \dfrac{A_j - \Delta T_j}{(1+i)^j} =$

$$\sum\limits_{j=1}^{n} \dfrac{\Delta T_j}{(1+i)^j}$$

P represents the value of the property prior to the new tax; P_t represents the value after the new tax. The difference between P and P_t--ΔP--will be affected by (1) the size of the new tax; (2) the duration of the new tax; and (3) the appropriate return to an investment having the taxed property's degree of risk and liquidity. The capitalized value of the change in future property taxes will equal $\sum\limits_{j=1}^{n} \dfrac{\Delta T_j}{(1+i)^j}$, assuming that the unexpected tax change may vary from year to year and that i remains unchanged during the relevant period. If the change is constant over time and continues forever, the capitalized value of the tax is simply $\Delta T/i$.

The above formulation assumes that the supply of property remains perfectly inelastic in the short run.

In other words, short-run changes in supply will in no way offset the change in the price of property caused by capitalization of property taxes.[1]

Further Tests for Capitalization

If tax capitalization actually occurs, tax increases should be inversely proportional to price decreases. Several methods were employed to test whether the expected relationship actually exists. The samples were first divided into several parts according to the size of the tax changes. Difference-in-means tests were then employed to see if price changes and tax changes grew proportionally. Price changes were also regressed on tax changes and the coefficients tested for significance. Finally, simple correlations between price changes and tax changes were calculated and tested for significance.

These tests are first applied to capitalization occurring between Periods I and II. Table A divides Sample II into thirds according to the size of the tax change, just as was done for Sample III in Table XXX. As the change in taxes (ΔT) becomes larger, the change in prices (ΔP) also grows larger. The difference in means for ΔP is significant at the 95 percent confidence level between the first and second thirds, at the 50 percent confidence level between the second and last thirds. Between the first and final thirds, the difference in ΔP means is significant at the 99 percent confidence level.

Results of the second test for property tax capitalization between Periods I and II are presented in *equation (2)*.

$$\Delta P = 6517.431 - 35.653 \; \Delta T \qquad R^2 = .264$$
$$(1240.808) \quad (5.235)$$

Though the low R^2 indicates that ΔT accounts for only a relatively small share of the variations in ΔP, the coefficient of ΔT is significant at the .001 level.[2]

TABLE A

MEASUREMENT OF TAX CAPITALIZATION OCCURRING BETWEEN PERIODS I AND II

(a) Portion of Sample II (thirds)	(b) Average ΔT	(c) Average ΔP	(d) Difference in ΔP means	(e) Confidence level for difference in ΔP means	(f)[1] Capitalization ratio
1st	$181	$- 446	$-1757	95 percent	2.5
2nd	232	-2203	- 389	50 percent	9.5
3rd	280	-2592			9.3
				Average	7.1

The confidence level for the difference in ΔP means between the first and last thirds is 98 percent.

Sample size = 131

[1](f) = -(c)/(b)

For the third test, calculation of the simple correlation coefficient between ΔP and ΔT yields a value of .5142, also significant at the .001 level. Thus all three tests provide consistent evidence that larger tax increases result in larger price reductions--a result that supports the theory of tax capitalization.

The Capitalization Ratio

Equation (2) estimates that for each $1 rise in taxes the selling price of a house fell by $35.65. A capitalization ratio of 35.6:1 seems extremely high, and due to the low R^2 it must be viewed with some skepticism. Fortunately the capitalization ratio can also be estimated by comparing the average ΔP with the average ΔT in Table A.

When Sample II is divided into thirds, $\Delta P/\Delta T$ ranges from 2.5 to 9.5. The average equals 7.1. If the tax increase is assumed to be permanent, a capitalization ratio of 7:1 implies an expected rate of return equal to 1/7, or 14.3 percent. Such capitalization ratio between Periods I and II appears low considering existing estimates of rates of return to residential dwellings. It may be attributed to incomplete capitalization of the tax change.

In order to determine whether further capitalization occurred between Periods II and III, the relationship between changes in taxes and changes in prices could be examined. A second method would be to compare the estimated change in price between Periods I and III with the change between Periods I and II. If for each dollar increase in taxes, prices are still further below the expected price (without the tax increase) in Period III than they were in Period II, then it would appear that the process of capitalization had not been fully completed by the end of Period II.

The expected price can be derived from *equation (3)*, which indicates the relationship between the sale price and both the assessed value and age of homes in Sample II.

$$P = -2829.69 + 5.153 \text{ S} + 106.636 \text{ A} \qquad R^2 = .580$$
$$(2911.60) \quad (.392) \qquad (41.215)$$

The standard error of the *equation (3)* regression is $3499, with the sale value of homes in the sample ranging from $18,000 to $71,500. Prices predicted by *equation (3)* are adjusted upward to take into account the 3.4 percent average annual increase in real estate prices in the surrounding Bay Area between April 1967 and April 1968.

Dividing Sample III into thirds according to the size of the tax increase, it appears that further capitalization did occur between Periods II and III. Table B indicates that higher taxes did result in lower prices, and that as the average ΔT increases, ΔP becomes more and more negative. Results of tests for variance between means show that the difference between mean ΔP's of the lowest and middle third and the middle and highest third are significant at less than 50 and the 95 percent confidence levels, respectively. The average capitalization ratio is about 6.5:1.

The other two tests do not contradict the conclusion that further tax capitalization occurred between Periods II and III. Regressing ΔP on ΔT yielded *equation (4)*.

$$\Delta P = 620.795 - 17.432 \; \Delta T \qquad R^2 = .049$$
$$(1967.225) \quad (8.175)$$

Again it is clear that other factors account for most of the variability in ΔP, but the coefficient of ΔT is significant at a .05 level. The simple correlation between ΔP and ΔT is .2217, significant at a .018 level. *Equation (4)* suggests that for each $1 rise in taxes prices fall by $17.43, but this must be interpreted with caution due to the extremely low R^2.

TABLE B

MEASUREMENT OF TAX CAPITALIZATION
OCCURRING BETWEEN PERIODS II AND III

(a) Portion of Sample III (thirds)	(b) Average ΔT	(c) Average ΔP	(d) Difference in ΔP means	(e) Confidence level for difference in ΔP means	(f)[1] Capitaliza- tion ratio
1st	$191	$- 633	$- 416	< 50 percent	3.3
2nd	229	-1049	-2280	95 percent	4.6
3rd	289	-3329			11.5
				Average	6.5

The confidence level for the difference in ΔP means
between the first and last thirds is 99 percent.

Sample size = 90

[1] (f) = - (c)/(b)

Another method of examining the tax capitalization that occurred between Periods II and III is to compare the capitalization between Periods I and II with that between I and III. Using *equation (1)* as a predictor of prices in Sample III, and making the appropriate adjustments for increases in real estate prices, it is possible to examine the total capitalization that occurred between Periods I and III. This was done in Table XXX, where it is evident that larger increases in taxes resulted in larger decreases in prices. The difference between ΔP means of the lowest and middle thirds was significant at a less than 50 percent confidence level, while that between the middle and highest thirds was significant at a 90 percent confidence level.

In *equation (5)* again the two other tests do not contradict this conclusion. ΔP regressed on ΔT yields

$$\Delta P = 3424.345 - 21.583 \ \Delta T \qquad R^2 = .075$$
$$(1945.028) \quad (8.082)$$

The coefficient of ΔT is significant at a .01 level. The simple correlation between ΔP and ΔT is .2738, significant at a .005 level.

When capitalization of the tax increase occurs over this longer period, Table XXX indicated that the capitalization ratio rises to 14.5 to 1. And *equation (5)* indicates that for each \$1 rise in taxes, prices will fall by \$21.58. But are these capitalization ratios reasonable? For a given rate of return and a constant tax change, the capitalized value of the tax change will be $\Delta T/i$. Since ΔP equals $\Delta T/i$, $i = \frac{\Delta T}{\Delta P}$. When the capitalization ratio is 14.5:1, solving for i yields $i = .069$. A capitalization ratio of 21.6 would yield $i = .046$. The capitalization ratio thus indirectly suggests that the rate of return on single-family housing in San Francisco lies between 4.6 and 6.9 percent. These rates of return are in fact quite consistent with the rates of return experienced by owners of duplexes and other apartments in San Francisco. From 1953 to 1964 rates of return in

San Francisco ranged from 8.6 percent experienced on
large apartment buildings to 6.8 percent on duplexes.[3]
Due to the satisfaction derived from homeownership,
rates of return on single-family dwellings might reasonably be expected to be below those on duplexes. Thus
these capitalization ratios do appear to be realistic.

One further note on capitalization ratios is in
order. Table A indicates that up to a point the ratio
$\Delta P/\Delta T$ increases as the size of the tax change increases.
Wicks, Little and Beck explain this phenomenon by sug-
gesting that the property with the smallest increases
becomes more desirable, resulting in some negative capitalization of the smallest tax increases.[4] In addition
home buyers may be more likely to notice large tax
increases. And because they fear that a trend toward
continually rising taxes is beginning, the large tax
increases may be overcapitalized.

Dummy Variables: Additional Evidence Concerning Capitalization and the Capitalization Ratio

If capitalization occurs, the price in Period II
should--for a given 1967 assessed value--be lower than
the price in Period I, other things remaining unchanged.
Since they are in no way related to actual selling prices
or the ages of the houses, the tax changes should be
expected to average about the same for all values of
homes.[5] It follows that capitalization of these tax
changes should cause an equal decline in the price of
homes over the entire range of values. Figure A shows
the expected relationship between assessed value and
actual sale price before and after the capitalization of
a tax change. Thus, the lines P(S) and P'(S) in Figure
A should be parallel. Further, given two properties with
equal 1967 assessed values, one sold in Period I, the
other in Period II, it should be anticipated that the
latter property would be sold at a lower price. This
hypothesis can be checked by employing a dummy variable
and combining Periods I and II into a single relationship, *equation (6)*.

FIGURE A

THE EXPECTED RELATIONSHIP BETWEEN ASSESSED VALUE AND THE ACTUAL SALE PRICE BEFORE AND AFTER THE CAPITALIZATION OF A TAX CHANGE

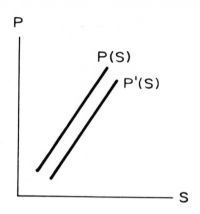

eq. (6):

$$P = \alpha + \beta_1 T + \beta_2 S + \beta_3 A$$

where P = the actual selling price
of the property
S = 1967 assessed value
A = the property's age
$T = \begin{cases} 0 \text{ in Period I} \\ 1 \text{ in Period II} \end{cases}$

Similarly, Periods II and III can be combined into a single relationship with T = 0 in Period II and T = 1 in Period III, and Periods I and III can be combined with T = 0 in Period I and T = 1 in Period III. The regression results for Samples I and II, II and III, and I and III are presented in *equations (7), (8)* and *(9)*.

eq. (7):
$$P = 44.286 - 1439.653 \ T + 5.044 \ S + 79.981 \ A$$
$$(455.069) \qquad (.291) \qquad (27.584) \qquad R^2 = .606$$

eq. (8):
$$P = 1218.914 - 697.121\ T + 4.497\ S + 95.252\ A \qquad R^2 = .521$$
$$(487.306) \qquad (.296) \qquad (29.007)$$

eq. (9):
$$P = 5992.070 - 1935.452\ T + 4.084\ S + 59.892\ A \qquad R^2 = .536$$
$$(495.948) \qquad (.309) \qquad (26.721)$$

Equation (9) indicates that for a given assessed value (S) and age (A) a parcel of property in Period III sold for $1935 less than in Period I even though homes with an average value of $30,300 in 1966 might normally have been expected to appreciate about $1468 (a 2.6 percent annual increase in prices). Thus if the tax change had not occurred, prices in Period III would have been approximately $3403 higher than they actually were. As tax increases on property sold in Period III average $236, the size of the price change suggests a capitalization ratio of approximately 3403:236, or 14.4:1.

Similar methods used to estimate the capitalization occurring between Periods I and II and Periods II and III produce capitalization ratio estimates of 7.8:1 and 6.6:1, respectively (see Table C). All three capitalization ratio estimates are consistent with the earlier estimates in this study.

The earlier estimates indicated an average fall in value of $3494 per home due to the higher property taxes. Both this and the estimate of $3403 suggest that single-family units declined an average of 11 to 12 percent in value due to the property tax increase.

TABLE C

DUMMY VARIABLE ESTIMATES OF CAPITALIZATION RATIOS

Time periods	Average ΔT	Average ΔP	Capitalization ratio
Period I to Period II	231	-1804	7.8:1
Period II to Period III	236	-1564	6.6:1
Period I to Period III	236	-3403	14.4:1

NOTES TO APPENDIX

1. For the case of single-family dwellings in the City of San Francisco, this should be a sufficiently realistic assumption.

2. In *equation (2)*, as well as in *equations (4)* and *(5)*, the positive constant indicates that prices of single-family dwellings would have increased if taxes had remained unchanged. However, only in the case of *equations (4)* and *(5)* are the constants significantly positive at above a 90 percent confidence level.

Examination of Samples II and III indicated that there are no identifiable exogenous variables that would cause ΔT and ΔP to vary simultaneously. If ΔT increased as P increased, it might well be expected that ΔT and ΔP would vary simultaneously. But this is not the case. Tax changes were regressed on selling prices and ages of houses for Samples II and III. The regression results were as follows:

Sample II: $\Delta T = 262.42 - .0005\ P - .509\ A \qquad R^2 = .008$
$\qquad\qquad (32.07)\ (.0008) \qquad (.567)$

Sample III: $\Delta T = 124.17 + .0029\ P + .841\ A \qquad R^2 = .100$
$\qquad\qquad (36.33)\ (.0030) \qquad (.887)$

No significant relationship appears to exist between the change in taxes and either the size of the selling price of the homes or the age of the homes.

3. Richard J. Recht and Louis K. Loewenstein, "Variations in Rates of Return," *The Appraisal Journal*, 33(2): 243-248 (1965).

4. See Wicks, Little and Beck, Ch. VI note 5, p. 264.

5. This suggests that this particular tax change increased the regressivity of the local tax structure. Owners of lower priced houses faced tax increases as large as did owners of higher priced homes. The tax increase, since it was regressive with respect to the value of homes, was also regressive with respect to the income of homeowners.

# VII

Taxation of Nonresidents

THE ISSUE

In 1967 the San Francisco Board of Supervisors adopted an income tax that applied to wages and salaries earned in San Francisco by nonresidents. Mayor Joseph Alioto justified the tax, claiming that the city provided commuters with services for which they did not pay. Commuters retorted that their revenue contributions, though to a large extent indirect, more than compensated for the city's services. Although a lower court ruled the "commuter" tax unconstitutional, the question of whether commuters pay their share of the core city's taxes remained unanswered.

Three students of urban finance--Lyle Fitch, Julius Margolis and David Davies--have taken positions partially supporting the claims of commuter groups.[1] They feel that the benefits provided to commuters are offset by the increased tax receipts that accompany them. But three other scholars--Amos Hawley, Harvey Brazer and Woo Sik Kee--have asserted that a growing suburban population increases the demands made on the core city and this in turn increases core city expenditures.[2] They stress the possibility that the suburban populations do not provide sufficient revenues to cover these additional costs.

The legitimacy of taxing nonresidents is an especially important question in this study, because seven of the 10 types of local income taxes considered would tax income earned within San Francisco by nonresidents. We

must ask whether the commuter should contribute more to
San Francisco tax revenues, and whether the tax receipts
accompanying the commuter are more or less than the
expenditures made to attract and serve him. The present
chapter seeks to shed additional light on this question
by estimating the share of local tax revenue paid by nonresidents as well as the share of public expenditures
benefiting them.

PUBLIC EXPENDITURES AND NONRESIDENTS

Nonresidents affect and are affected by city revenues and expenditures in several ways. They increase
the demand and thus the expenditures for public services
supplied by the City and County of San Francisco. They
benefit from any local tax reduction that lowers the
price of goods and services purchased in San Francisco.
And nonresidents who furnish factors of production (land,
labor, capital) to San Francisco business may benefit
from any tax reductions accruing to business.

On the other hand, if businesses are able to shift
taxes onto the consumer, nonresidents contribute to San
Francisco revenues whenever they purchase goods or services within the community. Further, if they furnish
factors of production to San Francisco businesses, they
pay San Francisco taxes whenever business is able to pass
a portion of these back on to suppliers of land, labor
or capital.

In order to weight these factors, it is necessary to
determine which public expenditures are actually attributable to residents alone, which are attributable to
residents and nonresidents alike. This may be done by
first allocating total public expenditures to two main
sectors: (1) those primarily attributable to the residential sectors of the community; and (2) those attributable to the business sectors. The second group may
then be theoretically separated into (a) the share of the
expenditures benefiting business that is received by nonresidents through their participation in business

activities, whether on the production or consumption side, and (b) the share that is received by residents through their participation in business activities.

Several attempts have been made to determine the portions of total public expenditures that benefit the business and the residential sectors of the community. (See Table XXXI) Services included in all these studies are public safety, public works and general government. Several of the studies were much more comprehensive: They included parking, utilities, capital improvement and parks. Among the categories of expenditure omitted were welfare, hospitals and schools. This is not to deny that business benefits from the existence of a public school system. However, schools are a major expenditure that would be necessary even if the community contained no business whatsoever.

These studies reveal a fairly consistent pattern of expenditures. For each city examined in Table XXXI, expenditures per acre are much greater on commercial than on industrial property, while expenditures on industrial property are somewhat in excess of those on residential property. Overall expenditures per acre on commercial property average 5.5 times those on residential property; the ratio of commercial to industrial property expenditures averages 3.9.

PUBLIC EXPENDITURES BENEFITING NONRESIDENTS:
THE CASE OF SAN FRANCISCO

Land Use in San Francisco

By employing San Francisco land-use data, public expenditures can be divided into those benefiting business and those benefiting residents. In 1964, 9037 acres in San Francisco County were used for residential purposes, and 1478 acres for commercial purposes. (See Table XXXII) Industry and utilities together use 2418 acres for what can be generally described as industrial purposes.

TABLE XXXI

EXPENDITURES PER ACRE
ACCORDING TO LAND USE FOR SELECTED CITIES

City	Use of land		
	Residential	Commercial	Industrial
Arlington, Va.[a]	$ 778 (1.00)	$3071 (3.95)	$ 955 (1.23)
New Rochelle, N.Y.[b]	1065 (1.00)	4167 (3.91)	1318 (1.24)
San Leandro, Calif.[c]	401 (1.00)	2083 (5.19)	421 (1.05)
West Hartford, Conn.[d]	420 (1.00)	3901 (9.29)	883 (2.10)
Yorktown, N.Y.[e]	121 (1.00)	617 (5.10)	No indus. land
	1.00	5.49	1.40

Expenditures included:

[a]Fire, police, sanitation, highways, utilities and general government.

[b]Fire, police, roads, parks, sanitation, health, capital improvement, the municipal garage and general government.

[c]Fire, police, public works, parking and general government.

[d]Fire, police, streets, sewers, refuse and general government.

[e]Fire, police, highways, parks, lighting and general government.

Sources: Peter B. Lund, "Municipal Costs Arising from Business and Industry" (unpublished Ph.D. dissertation, Department of Economics, University of California, Berkeley, 1967); Office of Planning, Arlington County, Va., *Fiscal Aspects of Land Use*, No. 3, pt. 2 (1957); Charles S. Adams, *Land Use and Municipal Finance*, Report no. 1 (West Hartford: 1960); New Rochelle Planning Board, *Land Use, Zoning, and Economic Analysis* (New Rochelle: 1951); Frederick P. Clark & Associates, *Town Development Plan: Town of Yorktown, N.Y.* (Rye: 1955) and *Land Use and Community Taxes: A Planning Program for the Northeast Section of Yorktown, N.Y.* (Rye: 1958).

TABLE XXXII

USE OF LAND IN SAN FRANCISCO IN 1964

Land use	Acres
Residence	9,037
Commerce	1,478
Industry	1,464 } 2,418
Utilities	954
Institutions	440
Public	6,594
Private recreation	364
Vacant	2,274

Source: San Francisco Department of City Planning, *The Use of Land in San Francisco* (October 1964).

San Francisco Expenditures
Benefiting the Business Community

Certain services provided by the City and County of San Francisco may be considered to benefit the business community directly. These include expenditures for general government, public safety, highways, sanitation and waste removal, the conservation of health, the municipal railway and civil defense. In addition, expenditures for recreation facilities are included because of their role in attracting shoppers, tourists and potential employees to the city. In 1966-1967 total expenditures for these services—which are listed separately in Table XXXIII—totaled $105 million.

Dividing these expenditures between the business and the residential communities requires drawing rather bold assumptions from Table XXXI: that expenditures per acre of commercially used land are 5.5 times as great as expenditures per acre of residential land, and 3.9 times as great as expenditures per acre of industrial land. Adopting this assumption, expenditures for the above services are $5110 per acre of residential land, $28,105 per acre of commercial land, and $7154 per acre of industrial

TABLE XXXIII

EXPENDITURES IN SAN FRANCISCO FOR SERVICES THAT IN PART
DIRECTLY BENEFIT THE BUSINESS COMMUNITY
1966-67

Direct benefit expenditures

General government	$ 23,585,457
Public safety	41,682,634
Highways	5,931,921
Sanitation and waste	6,403,483
Conservation of health	5,761,100
Recreation	11,953,544
Municipal railway	9,556,617
Civil defense	145,883
Subtotal	$105,020,639

Other expenditures

Hospitals	$ 16,988,394
Public welfare	84,074,483
Correction	4,603,728
Schools	72,354,115
Libraries	2,530,368
Bond redemptions and interest	14,440,511
Pensions and compensation	19,263,020
Judgments and losses	140,408
Capital additions from revenues	11,493,351
Miscellaneous, net	36,969
Subtotal	$225,925,347
TOTAL EXPENDITURES	$330,945,986

Source: Controller of the City and County of San Francisco, *Annual Report* for the fiscal year ending June 30,
1967, p. 4.

179

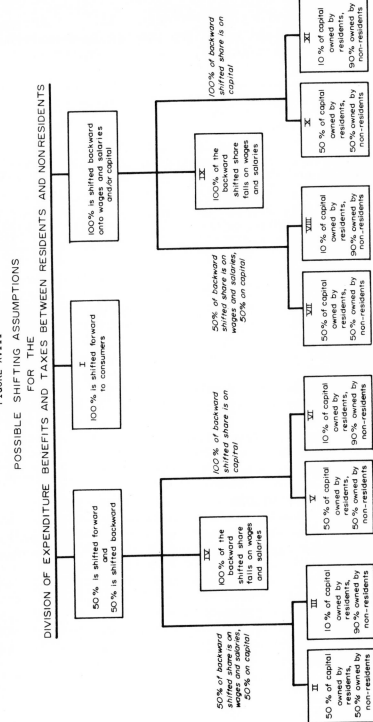

FIGURE XVIII

POSSIBLE SHIFTING ASSUMPTIONS
FOR THE
DIVISION OF EXPENDITURE BENEFITS AND TAXES BETWEEN RESIDENTS AND NON RESIDENTS

land. (See Appendix A for Chapter VII.) If these
figures are multiplied by the acreage in each category,
$41,539,190 of the $105 million spent on the items
listed may be attributed to commerce, $17,298,372 to
industry. In each case a share of the expenditures will
accrue to the benefit of nonresidents.

The Division Between Residents and Nonresidents
of Expenditures Benefiting the Business Community

To the extent that nonresidents are engaged in business activities within the community as customers,
employees, or business owners, they benefit from government services provided to the business sector. Like
residents, they benefit from the very existence of job
opportunities and from the marketplaces that accompany
normal business activities. But in order to allocate
these benefits between residents and nonresidents, it is
necessary to make a number of assumptions concerning the
ownership of capital in San Francisco; the division of
benefits between those passed forward to consumers and
those passed backward on to labor and capital; and the
division of the latter between labor and capital. The
sets of assumptions used in deriving the estimates are
outlined in Figure XVIII. They are basically the same as
those employed in estimating the spenders' welfare
effect. In this case, however, expenditure benefits are
being estimated, not tax reduction benefits.

Regardless of the choice of assumptions, local
government expenditures are assumed to accrue to the
benefit of customers, employees and owners of capital in
much the same way as a tax reduction. Thus if the city
did not provide police and fire protection, the business
community would pay the same amount or more to purchase
equivalent protection from some other source. Since the
business receives protection worth $1000 from the city,
it has $1000 that will flow to consumers through lower
prices, to employees through higher wages, or to owners
through increased returns on capital. Each of the other
expenditures considered has similar effects. Expenditures on recreation and the municipal railway may also

increase the supply of labor by making San Francisco a more desirable place to live and by broadening the area from which the business community can draw its labor supply.

Table XXXIV indicates that the total expenditures benefiting nonresidents are substantial.

LOCAL TAXES EXPORTED FROM THE CITY OF SAN FRANCISCO

San Francisco expenditures benefiting nonresidents are sizable. But to what extent do nonresidents pay for the public expenditure benefits they receive? In this section some approximate answers to this question are provided, utilizing the same sets of assumptions introduced when discussing the spenders' welfare effect.

Estimates of taxes exported by the City and County of San Francisco are presented in Table XXXIV. Depending on the assumptions employed, nonresidents paid between 23.6 and 34.9 percent of the $208,346,677 collected in fiscal 1966-1967.[3] Other tax exporting studies indicate that these are reasonable estimates. Charles McLure estimated:

> For the nation as a whole $10.2 billion or 25 per cent of all state and local taxes collected in 1962 were exported to nonresidents of the taxing state, according to short-run analysis. According to long-run analysis, $8.3 billion or 20 per cent of these taxes were exported. The export rates for individual states ranged from 17 per cent in South Dakota to 38 per cent in Delaware in the short run and from 15 per cent in Maine to 35 per cent in Delaware and Nevada in the long run.... All but eleven states export 19 to 23 per cent of their taxes in the short run. Similarly, in the long

TABLE XXXIV

ESTIMATED EXPENDITURE BENEFITS AND TAXES EXPORTED TO NONRESIDENTS

Case[a]	(1) Expenditures due to or benefiting nonresidents	(2) Taxes paid directly or indirectly by nonresidents	(3) Excess of taxes over expenditure benefits	(4)[b] Percent of total taxes exported
I	$34,541,177	$ 69,490,368	$34,949,191	33.4
II	29,474,357	59,307,293	29,832,936	28.5
III	35,537,114	71,144,454	35,607,340	34.2
IV	26,975,936	54,276,498	27,300,562	26.1
V	31,974,530	64,338,086	32,363,556	30.9
VI	43,740,042	88,012,408	44,272,366	42.2
VII	24,413,438	49,124,219	24,710,781	23.6
VIII	36,178,950	72,798,541	36,619,591	34.9
IX	19,413,096	39,062,631	19,649,535	18.7
X	29,413,782	59,185,806	29,772,024	28.4
XI	52,944,807	106,534,450	53,589,643	51.1

[a]See Figure XVIII.

[b](4) = (2)/$208,346,677

Source: See Appendix B for data sources and methods of estimation.

run only ten states export more
than 24 per cent of their taxes
or less than 16 per cent.[4]

Earlier tax studies in Michigan, Wisconsin and Minnesota
estimated that 21 to 33 percent of all state and local
taxes were exported.[5] In addition, a study of the incidence of local taxes in New York City estimated that 25.1
percent of all local taxes were exported to nonresidents.[6]

The rough estimates in Table XXXIV all indicate that
nonresidents contribute considerable revenue to the tax
coffers of San Francisco. In fact, nonresidents appear
to contribute more in tax revenues than they receive in
benefits. The difference ranges from $29,832,936 to
$53,589,643.

Poverty-Linked Expenditures

But this evidence may not satisfy those who feel
that the core city provides more than job opportunities
and shopping centers for nonresidents. Still others may
feel that even if the core city is the most likely place
for ethnic minority groups, the poor and the uneducated
to congregate, this is no reason for placing the entire
burden of the resulting welfare expenditures on city
residents alone. This line of argument is worthy of
consideration.

Expenditures for hospitals, public welfare,
libraries and correction were not included in those
previously considered. In 1966-1967 expenditures for
these items amounted to $108,196,973. Whether nonresi-
dents should pay more than they do may depend on the
disparity between core-city and suburban expenditures on
"poverty-linked" items. Where this disparity is particularly large, it can be argued that the suburbs should
help the central city meet its burdens.

Comparison with Other Metropolitan Areas

A study based on 1962 figures, by Woo Sik Kee, compares city and suburban poverty-linked expenditures per capita in 22 metropolitan areas. It indicates that the city/suburb disparity is considerably less in the San Francisco metropolitan area than in other large metropolitan areas.[7] In 1962 it was approximately $6.[8] This would seem to indicate that there is less disparity in living conditions between the core city of San Francisco and its suburbs than in other metropolitan areas and that poverty-linked expenditures have been more widely dispersed among other local budgets. Had the small existing disparity been covered entirely by nonresidents, it would have amounted to an expenditure of approximately $4.5 million. Yet the data developed for 1966-1967 suggest that nonresidents contributed far more than this amount to poverty-linked expenditures in San Francisco. Thus San Francisco has little reason to demand still more assistance from nonresidents on the ground that they are undertaxed.

CONCLUSION

The fact that local income taxes are not currently employed by any of the central cities in California may indicate that the cities have felt neither the overwhelming need to draw additional revenues from the surrounding suburbs, nor justification for requiring non-residents to contribute a larger share of central city revenues. In the metropolitan areas of the East and Midwest, the disparity between per capita poverty-linked expenditures in the cities and in the suburbs is much greater than in California metropolitan areas. Cities in these other states may well have a greater need to look beyond their borders for revenues. The suburbs of those cities, recognizing the struggle that the core cities have to maintain their health and the benefits that suburbs derive from the cities, might be expected to show greater willingness to contribute additional revenues to the central city treasuries.

The findings of this paper lend support to Lyle Fitch's assertion that:

> We should be wary of concluding...
> that the suburbs are a net burden
> to the central city, or that there
> is typically an imbalance in the
> capacities of central cities and
> aggregate suburban governments to
> meet their expenditure need, which
> needs redress.[9]

Compared to many other cities, San Francisco should feel little need to alter the tax structure so that non-residents pay a larger share of total taxes. In fact, nonresidents can make a strong case for their claim that they currently contribute more than their share of San Francisco's tax revenues.

NOTES TO CHAPTER VII

1. Lyle C. Fitch, "Discussion," *American Economic Review*, 58(2): 328-330 (1958); Julius Margolis, "Municipal Fiscal Structure in a Metropolitan Region," *Journal of Political Economy*, 65(3): 225-236 (1957); David Davies, "Financing Urban Functions and Services," in R.O. Everett and R.H. Leach, eds., *Urban Problems and Prospects* (Dobbs Ferry, N.Y.: Oceana Publications, 1965), pp. 119-153.

2. Amos H. Hawley, "Metropolitan Population and Municipal Government Expenditures in Central Cities," *Journal of Social Issues*, 7(1,2): 100-108 (1951); Harvey E. Brazer, "The Role of Major Metropolitan Centers in State and Local Finance," *American Economic Review*, 48(2): 305-317 (1958); *City Expenditures in the United States*, National Bureau of Economic Research Occasional Paper 66 (New York: 1959); Woo Sik Kee, "Central City Expenditures and Metropolitan Areas," *National Tax Journal*, 18(4): 337-353 (1965); Kee, "City-Suburban Differentials in Local Government Fiscal Effort," *National Tax Journal*, 21(2): 183-189 (1968).

3. Tax collections in San Francisco for the fiscal year 1966-67 were as follows:

Property taxes and penalties	$183,622,600
Retail purchase and use tax	21,151,747
Hotel room tax	1,866,229
Other taxes and licenses	1,706,101
	$208,346,677

4. Charles McLure, "Tax Exporting in the U.S.: Estimates for 1962," *National Tax Journal*, 20(1): 49-77 (1967), see especially pp. 64 and 66.

5. See O.H. Brownlee, Ch. V note 4, p. 1; R.A. Musgrave and Darwin Daicoff, Ch. V note 4, p. 135; and

University of Wisconsin Tax Impact Study Committee, Ch.
V note 4, p. 46.

6.   See Alan D. Donheiser, Ch. V note 4, p. 162.

7.   See Woo Sik Kee, "City-Suburban Differentials...," note 2 above, especially pp. 184-185. In
poverty-linked expenditures he included local government
expenditures for public welfare, health and hospital services, and expenditures for the education of children in
families with incomes under $3000. For the 22 largest
U.S. metropolitan areas, the disparity in these per
capita expenditures between cities and suburbs ranged
from $44.72 in Newark to -$2.17 in San Diego.

8.   This compares with a $31 disparity in St. Louis
and New York, a $35 disparity in Boston and Cincinnati,
and a $45 disparity in Newark. St. Louis, Cincinnati and
New York use local income taxes to collect revenues from
nonresidents. (Kee, loc. cit.)

9.   See Fitch, note 1 above, p. 328.

Appendix A

CALCULATIONS OF EXPENDITURES PER ACRE OF LAND

Total expenditures considered equal $105,020,639.

Expenditures per acre of commercial property are estimated to be 5.5 times those per acre of residential property.

Expenditures per acre of industrial property are estimated to be 1.4 times those on residential property.

Therefore, if x = expenditure per acre of residential property, then $9037x + 1478(5.5)x + 2418(1.4)x = 105,020,639$ and $x = 5110$.

Expenditures per acre on residential property equal $5110.

Expenditures per acre on commercial property equal 5.5(x) or $28,105.

Expenditures per acre on industrial property equal 1.4(x) or $7154.

Appendix B

METHOD USED TO ESTIMATE THE DIVISION BETWEEN RESIDENTS AND NONRESIDENTS OF EXPENDITURES BENEFITING BUSINESS AND TAX PAYMENTS MADE BY BUSINESS

Expenditures Benefiting Business

In the case where 50 to 100 percent of the expenditure benefit or the tax change is shifted forward, the percentage of sales going to nonresidents must be estimated. Estimates made in Chapter V, using the method developed by Homer Hoyt,[1] indicated that 59 percent of the sales of commercial enterprises and 58 percent of the sales of industrial enterprises went to nonresidents.

Similarly, for those cases in which 50 to 100 percent of the expenditure benefit or tax is passed backward, the percentage of nonresident employees must be estimated. Estimates based on U.S. census data, California Department of Employment data, and a 1968 industrial survey by the Greater San Francisco Chamber of Commerce indicated that for both the commercial enterprises and the industrial enterprises 33 percent of the employees were nonresidents. In considering taxes and expenditure benefits passed backwards on to capital, two cases are examined: (1) with the assumption that 90 percent of the capital is owned by nonresidents, and (2) with the assumption that 50 percent is owned by nonresidents.

With the above information, the distribution of benefits to nonresidents was made as follows:

Benefits = commercial benefits passed forward + industrial benefits passed forward + commercial benefits passed back to owners of capital + commercial benefits passed back to labor + industrial benefits passed back k

---

[1] Op. cit., Hoyt and Weimer, Ch. V, App. A note 1.

to owners of capital + industrial benefits passed back to labor.

For Case II the following calculations were made:

Benefits = $(.59)(.5)(41,529,190) + (.58)(.5)(17,298,372) + (.5)^3(41,539,190) + (.5)^2(.33)(41,539,190) + (.5)^3(17,298,372) + (.5)^2(17,298,372)(.33) = $29,474.357.

Tax Payments Made by Business

Tax payments made by businesses in San Francisco for fiscal year 1966-67 were as follows:

Property taxes:
Commercial properties	(.32)(183,722,603)	$58,759,232
Industrial and utility properties	(.19)(183,722,603)	$34,888,295
Retail purchase and use tax		$21,151,747
Hotel room tax		$ 1,866,229
Other taxes and licenses		$ 1,706,108

For the purpose of the following calculations it is assumed that the sales tax, the hotel room tax, and all other taxes and licenses are paid by commercial enterprises and that industrial enterprises pay only the property tax. The commercial enterprises, then, pay a total of $83,483,316 in local taxes, while the industrial and utility enterprises pay only $34,888,295. The division of these taxes between residents and nonresidents was made as follows, with the figures presented below equaling the amounts paid by nonresidents.

Tax payments = commercial tax payment passed forward + industrial tax payment passed forward + commercial tax payment passed back to owners of capital + commercial tax payment passed back to labor + industrial tax payment passed back to owners of capital + industrial tax payment passed back to labor.

For Case II the following calculations were made:

Tax payments $= (.59)(.5)(83,483,316) + (.58)(.5)$ $(34,888,295) + (.5)^3(83,483,316) + (.33)(.5)^2(83,483,316)$ $+ (.5)^3(34,888,295) + (.33)(.5)^2(34,888,295) =$ $\underline{\$59,307,293}$.

Similar calculations were made for all the other 10 cases.

VIII

Summary and Conclusion

Local income taxes have received increasing attention in California and the Bay Area, as well as in other
metropolitan areas of the country. However, even in
those communities that have adopted local income taxes,
scant analysis of their effects has preceded their adoption. The intent of this study is twofold: first to
provide a framework that can be used to examine the
effects of local income taxes in other communities; and,
second, to examine the probable effects of several types
of local income taxes for the City and County of San
Francisco.*

LOCAL INCOME TAXES AS A NEEDED AND
RELIABLE SOURCE OF REVENUE

Government expenditures in metropolitan areas have
been increasing at a very rapid rate. In the case of San
Francisco, property tax rates have been rising rapidly in
an attempt to keep up with the mounting expenditures of
local government. An additional revenue-raising measure,
if it meets certain basic requirements, would be most
welcome.

---

* This chapter was also published as "Local Income Taxes
as an Alternative to Higher Property Taxes: A Summary,"
Public Affairs Report, 11(4) (Berkeley: Institute of
Governmental Studies, University of California, 1970).

Local income taxes are already in effect in Pennsylvania, Ohio, New York, Missouri, Kentucky, Michigan, Maryland, Alabama and New Mexico, and have been found to be reliable sources of revenue. Evidence from many communities indicates that local income taxes have helped to hold down property tax rates. In addition, local income tax revenues automatically rise as incomes rise. This response of revenues to changes in income is greater for income taxes than for the more traditional local tax forms. Thus, use of local income taxation can make it less difficult for cities to raise revenues to meet their continually rising expenditure needs. Both rates and bases differ markedly from one city to another. Tax rates range from .5 percent to 2.5 percent on individual income tax bases, while local income taxes on corporate profits range from 0 percent in Baltimore to 5.5 percent in New York City.

Administrative and Compliance Costs

Studies have indicated that the administrative costs of collecting local income taxes do not differ significantly from the costs of collecting other local taxes. The compliance costs of income taxes should be, however, of greater concern. Compliance costs include the actual expense to businesses of complying with local income tax regulations, as well as the out-of-pocket expense paid by individual citizens in order to get the tax forms completed, and the opportunity costs of spending the time preparing this additional tax form. Businesses operating in jurisdictions with local income taxes have complained about the costs of complying with local income tax ordinances, and have pointed out that the costs of complying are frequently in excess of the taxes paid. Many corporations operating in more than one local jurisdiction have refrained from filing tax returns in all but their home jurisdictions.

By using flat-rate taxes on wages and salaries which can easily be withheld by employers, or by using a tax base similar to or identical to that used for the state

income tax, compliance costs can be held to an acceptable
level. On the other hand, evidence suggests that compliance costs for more complex forms of local income taxes
may be significant.

Effects Upon Location Decisions

Local income taxes, in general, appear to have had
little effect on the decisions of businesses and households concerning location. If evidence is to be found
concerning the decisions of corporations on most favorable locations, it would be worthwhile to examine the
developments in New York City. The 5.5 percent local tax
levy on corporate net profits in New York City is at
least three times as high as the corporate profits tax
levied by any other local government.

THE EFFECTS OF LOCAL INCOME TAXES ON THE DISTRIBUTION
OF REAL INCOME AND WEALTH WITHIN A COMMUNITY

How would the movement toward local income taxes
affect the distribution of income and wealth in the community? In order to examine this issue, it was assumed
that all the revenues collected through a local income
tax would be used to lower property tax rates. This
assumption appears to be reasonably well founded because
property tax rates have traditionally been set in order
to fill the gap between other revenues and the anticipated expenditures of the city. Therefore, an additional
source of revenue, a local income tax, would permit
property tax rates to be reduced.

In order to state the conclusions as clearly and
concisely as possible, most of the following statements
pertain to only one of the types of local income taxes
examined--a flat-rate tax. This tax form would levy a
one percent tax on (a) the earned and unearned income of
San Francisco residents, (b) the income earned by nonresidents in San Francisco, and (c) corporate net profits
arising in San Francisco. The broad base and flat rate

of this tax make its general appeal greater than some of
the other forms considered if San Francisco were independently to enact a local income tax.

The other local income taxes considered range from
a flat-rate tax levied solely on the earned income of
residents (the least progressive) to a tax levied as a 50
percent supplement to the California state individual
income tax (the most progressive). The supplement would
entail (a) levying a tax on the tax base used by the
state; (b) establishing the rate as half that set by the
state; and (c) arranging for the state to collect the
revenues for the local government. (This arrangement
exists between the city of Baltimore and the state of
Delaware.)

The Effect of the Tax Change on Homeowners

If revenues raised by an income tax are used to
reduce property tax rates, most individuals owning homes
in San Francisco would experience a decrease in overall
local taxes. For the flat-rate tax being considered,
only those homeowners in high-income classes (generally
homeowners with high incomes relative to the value of
their homes) would experience an overall increase in
local taxes.

Homeowners living on low fixed incomes, or incomes
exempt from a local income tax, would benefit from the
tax change. Thus substitution of income tax for property
tax revenues is one way in which relief could be provided
to retired homeowners and others living on low fixed
incomes. Even the adoption of a flat-rate local income
tax levied only on the earned income of residents would
permit a reduction in property taxes that would benefit
many homeowners with the lowest incomes.

If the homeowners were the only residents in a community it appears that the tax change would have a significant progressive influence on the local tax structure.

The Long-Run and Short-Run Effects
of the Tax Change on Renters

In San Francisco, renters compose an even larger segment of the population than do homeowners. In 1960, according to the *U.S. Census of Housing*, 65 percent of all households in San Francisco rented their housing, and the construction trend since that time would indicate that the percentage of renters is even greater in 1970.

For renters, the short-run effects of the tax change differ markedly from those in the long run. The short run does not allow sufficient time for the supply of housing to be affected by the lower property taxes. In the short run, therefore, the adoption of the flat-rate tax, or any other form of local income tax without exemptions and deductions, would increase the local tax bill of nearly all renters. And with a given supply of housing, and a given demand for housing, there is no reason why rents should fall. In fact, it might be several years before renters would experience the full benefits of an increased supply of housing brought about by lower property taxes. This is particularly important for cities such as San Francisco with relatively large numbers of renters.

In the long run, lower property taxes would lead to an increase in the supply of housing. This larger supply of housing would lead to lower rents for a given level of demand. Many low-income renters, in the long run, would find that the lower rents made possible by the reduced property taxes would more than compensate for the local income taxes they pay.

On the other hand, for each of the local income taxes considered, many renters in the middle- and upper-income classes would find that rent reductions resulting from the lower property taxes would not fully compensate for the income tax payments. Also, in the long run, whatever the form of local income tax adopted, if the revenues were used to reduce property tax rates the average homeowner in any given income class would benefit

more than the average renter simply because the homeowner consumes more housing.

Renters: Low-Income and Nonwhite

In 1960, 78 percent of all households in San Francisco with incomes below $5000 rented their dwellings.
Hence, in the short run, 78 percent of those with incomes
below $5000 would pay local income taxes, would not pay
less in other forms of taxation, and would receive no
more benefits from public expenditures than before. As
stated, it might take years for the housing market to
adjust; during this period, the majority of the poor
households in San Francisco would be paying more in taxes
to the city, without a sufficient fall in the price of
housing to compensate for the higher taxes.

Negroes and other nonwhite groups in cities have
traditionally been renters. In addition, many in these
minority groups have had low incomes. In San Francisco
in 1960, 75 percent of all nonwhite households rented
their housing and 68 percent of those who rented had
incomes below $5000. For all but the most progressive
type of local income tax, the use of the income tax
revenues to reduce property tax rates would adversely
affect the vast majority of San Francisco's nonwhite
population, many of whom are poor.

THE INCOME EFFECT AND VERTICAL EQUITY

The politically sensitive (or not so sensitive)
policymakers may wish to adopt some form of local income
tax which would avoid much of the adverse effect on
renters. The inclusion of adequate deductions and exemptions within the local tax ordinance would go far in
eliminating this short-run effect.

Only one of the tax forms considered employed progressive rates and allowed for exemptions and deductions:
the supplement to the California state individual income

tax. Without exemptions and deductions, the introduction
of a flat-rate local income tax would do little to change
the essential regressivity of the local tax structure.
In the long run, the regressivity of the local tax structure would be slightly ameliorated with the introduction
of the flat-rate tax on income (see Table XXXV). This
slight influence may not be sufficient to motivate the
policymaker to push for the adoption of this new form of
tax.

The progressive influence exerted by a local income
tax could be increased in several ways. First, including
exemptions in the local tax ordinance would further
increase the long-run progressive influence of a local
income tax. Second, a stronger progressive influence on
the tax structure would be exerted if a supplement to the
state income tax were adopted. However, any meaningful
supplement to the California personal income tax, if
levied independently by San Francisco, would be likely to
affect adversely the location decisions of high-income
households. For example, a 50 percent supplement would
have yielded only $23 million in 1967 compared with $186
million yielded by the property tax. Such a supplement--
offset by equal property tax reductions--would still
leave the local tax structure highly regressive. Third,
if local income taxes were levied at flat rates higher
than those considered in this study, and if the income
tax revenues were used to reduce property tax rates, the
progressive influence of the income tax would be greater.
But as with the supplement to the state income tax, the
effect of high local income tax rates on location decisions would make such taxes feasible only if levied on a
regional or statewide basis.

The local policymaker will be continually confronted
with the conflicting goals of (a) minimizing the locational effects of a local income tax; (b) reducing the
regressivity of the local tax structure; and (c) raising
sufficient revenues to carry on the activities of local
government. If local tax structures are to become
markedly less regressive or even progressive, changes
affecting the local tax structure will have to occur
either on a regional or statewide basis.

TABLE XXXV

PROPERTY TAX PAYMENT AS A PERCENT OF INCOME
BEFORE THE TAX CHANGE; AND PROPERTY TAXES PLUS LOCAL
INCOME TAXES[a] AS A PERCENT OF INCOME AFTER THE TAX
CHANGE IN (1) THE SHORT RUN AND (2) THE LONG RUN
IN SAN FRANCISCO, 1967

Money income before taxes	Taxes as a percent of money income for renters and homeowners combined		
	Before the tax change	After the tax change	
		Short run	Long run
	(percent)	(percent)	(percent)
$ 3,354	5.1	5.4	4.8
4,902	3.5	4.1	3.6
6,450	3.3	3.9	3.4
7,804	3.0	3.6	3.3
9,675	3.0	3.6	3.3
12,642	2.7	3.2	3.0
17,415	2.5	3.1	2.9
35,217	2.0	2.5	2.3

[a]A one percent tax levied on (a) all earned and
unearned income of residents, (b) all income earned in
San Francisco by nonresidents, and (c) corporate net
profits arising in San Francisco.

Before determining what type of local income tax, if any, would be desirable, the policymaker must consider at least two other effects of the tax change in order to get a true picture of the change's influence on the distribution of wealth and income in the community.

THE EFFECT OF PRICE CHANGES
UPON REAL INCOME OF RESIDENTS

In order to improve the estimates of the effects of the tax change on the real income of the individuals after the change, the "spenders' welfare effect" was considered. This effect relates to influence of tax change on the prices of goods, services and factors of production. In the case of San Francisco, for each of the types of income tax examined, it was found that the use of income tax revenues to lower property tax rates would reduce the amount of taxes that businesses would pay directly to the local government. (This is due to the fact that business property in San Francisco, as in all large cities, is a large part of total taxable property.) The increased after-tax revenues of businesses would either be passed on to consumers of goods and services or to the owners of factors of production. Such revenues may be passed on to consumers through lower prices, or they may be passed on to factors of production through increased wages, salaries, or returns to invested capital. Under various sets of assumptions, estimates were made concerning the extent to which each income class would benefit from the higher after-tax profits experienced by businesses. The inclusion of the spenders' welfare effect modifies in one major way the conclusions reached concerning the effects of the tax change upon the distribution of income in the community: Under several of the sets of assumptions, those individuals with high incomes are significantly less adversely affected by the adoption of a form of local income tax when the spenders' welfare effect is included. The progressive influence of a local income tax is even less than it appeared before the inclusion of the spenders' welfare effect.

PROPERTY TAX CAPITALIZATION AND
THE DISTRIBUTION OF WEALTH

This study has also been concerned with the effects that the use of local income tax revenues to reduce property tax rates would have upon the distribution of wealth in the community. This included a study of tax capitalization related to properties in San Francisco. The evidence indicates that for a certain set of demand conditions, for each unexpected dollar increase in the property taxes, the sales value of the home fell by about $14.50. This evidence suggests that for each unexpected $1 reduction in property taxes the sale value of a home would increase about $14.50. If the imposition of an income tax were to allow a significant reduction in property tax rates, those individuals owning residential property would experience a significant rise in their wealth. For some types of housing, the increase in the demand for housing due to a reduction in the amount of property taxes might be partially offset by the effect that the tax change would have upon after-tax income. Since those individuals with high incomes would be most likely to experience a reduction in their after-tax income, homes of high-income individuals might not rise in price by as much as other homes.

In any case, the capitalization of lower property taxes would not increase the wealth of the 65 percent of renting householders in the same way that it would increase the wealth of homeowners. The households that would not benefit from the capitalization of lower property taxes would include the 78 percent of those renters with incomes below $5000 in 1960; a component of this nonbenefiting group would be the 75 percent of all non-white households in San Francisco that were renting. The capitalization that would result from the lower property taxes made possible by the adoption of a local income tax would increase the wealth of those with higher incomes and/or already possessing considerable wealth. This evidence concerning tax capitalization may temper enthusiasm for reducing property taxes by substituting local income taxes. The inclusion of deductions and exemptions in the local tax ordinance would do nothing to compensate renters for the windfall gain that homeowners would experience.

It should be stressed that tax capitalization, and its attendant effect on the distribution of wealth, is a factor deserving careful consideration by policymakers.

THE TAXATION OF NONRESIDENTS: SOME COMMENTS

One of the facets of local income taxes to which policymakers have been attracted is the ability to tax those who work in the city, but do not live in the city. Local politicians could be excused for their attraction to this form of tax, since the taxation of constituents could always be expected to lose more votes than the taxation of those who are not constitutents. In some cases, it may be true that nonresidents already pay what could be considered their share into the central city's coffers, through the shifting of taxes forward onto goods purchased by nonresidents and backward onto factors of production supplied by nonresidents. The evidence examined in this study indicates that San Francisco may be one such case.

The fact that local income taxes are not currently employed by any of the central cities in California may indicate that the cities have felt neither the overwhelming need to draw additional revenues from the surrounding suburbs, nor justification for requiring nonresidents to contribute a larger share to central city revenues. In the metropolitan areas of the East and Midwest, the disparity between per capita poverty-linked expenditures in the cities and in the suburbs is much greater than in the California metropolitan areas. Cities in these other states may well have a greater need to look beyond their borders for revenues. And the suburbs of those cities, recognizing the real struggle that the core cities are having to maintain their health and the benefits that suburbs derive from healthy core cities, might be expected to show a greater willingness to contribute additional revenues to the central city treasuries.

CONCLUSIONS

For the student or policymaker interested in reducing regressivity in local tax structures, the findings and conclusions of this study are not as optimistic as one might wish. The evidence concerning the vertical equity of a local income tax in San Francisco does not lead to clear-cut conclusions. This is the result of three factors. First, for the tax change in which local income tax revenues would be used to reduce property tax rates, most renters would be adversely affected in the short run. Since the majority of renters have low incomes, if exemptions are not included in the local tax ordinance, the adoption of the new form of taxation would add little or nothing to the progressivity of the local tax structure in the short run. However, if only the income effect is considered in the long run, most forms of local income taxation would reduce the regressivity of the local tax structure so long as the income tax revenues are used to reduce property tax rates.

Second, the spenders' welfare effect may significantly influence the distribution of after-tax income, but the size of this effect for each income class cannot be confidently predicted. If conditions were such that the benefit of the lower property taxes on business accrues largely to the owners of capital in San Francisco, the income tax may have little effect upon the progressivity or regressivity of the local tax structure.

Third, capitalization of the lower property taxes would occur, and in order to determine how this capitalization would affect the distribution of wealth and income, a complete record of the owners of each type of property in San Francisco would be needed. This information is not available.

At least one other factor should be noted by policymakers who may be considering forms of local income taxation. It is not clear in all cases that a greater contribution to city revenues should be asked of nonresidents.

 **SELECTIVE BIBLIOGRAPHY**

GOVERNMENT PUBLICATIONS

California Council on Intergovernmental Relations. *Alternative Fiscal Models for Tax and Revenue Sharing in California: A Report.* Sacramento: January 1969.

California Franchise Tax Board. *Annual Report.* Sacramento: 1958 to 1966.

California. Legislature. Assembly. Interim Committee on Revenue and Taxation. *Financing Local Government in California.* Vol. IV, No. 3. Sacramento: 1964.

The Sales Tax. Vol. IV, No. 11. Sacramento: 1964.

Taxation of Property in California. Vol. IV, No. 12. Sacramento: 1964.

California. Legislature. Senate. *Report of the Senate Fact Finding Committee on Revenue and Taxation.* Parts 2, 3, 4 and 9. Sacramento: 1965.

City and County of San Francisco. Board of Supervisors. *San Francisco Tax Study.* (Report prepared by Arthur D. Little, Inc.). San Francisco: July 1967. Pp. 96-110.

City and County of San Francisco. Controller. *Annual Report of the Controller of the City and County of San Francisco.* San Francisco: 1958 to 1968.

Michigan. State Legislature, Regular Session of 1964. *Public and Local Acts*, "Act Number 284," pp. 537-556.

Minnesota. *Report of the Governor's Minnesota Tax Committee, 1956*. Minneapolis: Colwell Press, 1956.

New York. *Report of the New York State Commission for the Revision of the Tax Law*. Memos No. 4 and No. 5. Albany: 1932.

Ohio Municipal League.
First Revised Model Income Tax Ordinance. Columbus: October 1959.

Staff Report Number 3: Statistical Data--Property and Income Taxes, Rates, Collections and Valuations. Columbus: n.d.

Statistics on Municipal Income Taxes in Ohio. Columbus: May 1967.

Pennsylvania. Bureau of Municipal Affairs, Department of Internal Affairs. *The Local Tax Enabling Act of 1965*. Harrisburg: 1966.

U.S. Advisory Commission on Intergovernmental Relations. *The Commuter and the Municipal Income Tax*. Washington, D.C.: April 1970.

Local Nonproperty Taxes and the Coordinating Role of the State. Washington, D.C.: 1961.

State and Local Finances, Significant Features, 1966 to 1969. Washington, D.C.: November 1968.

State and Local Taxes, Significant Features, 1968. Washington, D.C.: January 1968.

Tax Overlapping in the United States, 1961. Washington, D.C.: 1961.

Tax Overlapping in the United States, 1964. Report M-23. Washington, D.C.: 1964.

U.S. Congress. House. Committee on the Judiciary.
  *Report of the Special Subcommittee on State Taxation
  of Interstate Commerce*. Report No. 1480. 88th Cong.,
  2d sess. Washington, D.C.: 1964. Chapter 14, "Local
  Corporate Income Taxes."

U.S. Department of Commerce. Bureau of the Census.
  City Government Finances in 1966-67. Washington, D.C.:
  1968.

U.S. Department of Labor. Bureau of Labor Statistics.
  Survey of Consumer Expenditures and Income, 1960-61.
  Report No. 237. Washington, D.C.

Wisconsin. Legislative Reference Bureau. *Municipal
  Income Taxation*. Informational Bulletin 66-6.
  Madison: 1966.

BOOKS

Bloom, Clark C. *State and Local Tax Differentials and
  the Location of Manufacturing*. Iowa City: State
  University of Iowa, 1956.

Brazer, Harvey E. *City Expenditures in the United
  States*. National Bureau of Economic Research Occasional Paper 66. New York: National Bureau of Economic Research, 1959.

Brazer, Harvey E., ed. *Michigan Tax Study: Staff
  Papers*. Lansing: 1958.

Brown, Harry Gunnison. *The Economics of Taxation*. New
  York: Henry Holt and Company, 1924.

Commerce Clearing House, Inc.
  *New York City--New Taxes on Corporations--Law and
  Explanation*. Chicago: 1966.

  *New York City--New Taxes on Individuals and Unincor-
  porated Businesses--Law and Explanation*. Chicago:
  1966.

Commerce Clearing House, Inc.
New York City--Personal Income Tax. Chicago: 1966.

de Vito de Marco, Antonio. *First Principles of Public
Finance*. New York: Harcourt, Brace and Company, Inc.,
1936.

Fisher, Ernest M. *Urban Real Estate Markets: Characteristics and Financing*. New York: National Bureau of
Economic Research, 1951.

Fisher, Ernest M. and Robert M. *Urban Real Estate*. New
York: Henry Holt and Company, 1954.

Floyd, Joe Summers, Jr. *Effects of Taxation on Industrial Location*. Chapel Hill: University of North
Carolina Press, 1952.

Goode, Richard. *The Individual Income Tax*. Washington,
D.C.: Brookings, 1964.

Haig, Robert M. and Carl S. Shoup. *The Financial Problem
of the City of New York*. A Report to the Mayor's Committee on Management Survey. New York: June 1952.

Jensen, Jens P. *Property Taxation in the United States*.
Chicago: University of Chicago Press, 1931.

Kimmel, Lewis H. *Taxes and Economic Incentives*. Washington, D.C.: Brookings, 1950.

McCracken, Paul W., ed. *Taxes and Economic Growth in
Michigan*. Kalamazoo: W.E. Upjohn Institute for
Employment Research, 1960.

Morgan, James N., et al. *Income and Welfare in the
United States*. New York: McGraw-Hill, 1962.

Morton, Walter A. *Housing Taxation*. Madison: University of Wisconsin Press, 1955.

Mueller, Eva, Arnold Wilken, and Margaret Wood. *Location Decisions and Industrial Mobility in Michigan.* Ann Arbor: Institute for Social Research, University of Michigan, 1961.

Musgrave, Richard A. *The Theory of Public Finance.* New York: McGraw-Hill, 1959.

Netzer, Dick.
The Economics of the Property Tax. Washington, D.C.: Brookings, 1966.

Impact of the Property Tax: Effect on Housing, Urban Land Use, Local Government Finance. Prepared for the Consideration of the National Commission on Urban Problems. Research Report No. 1. Washington, D.C.: 1968.

Quinto, Leon Jay. *Municipal Income Taxation in the United States.* Finance Project Technical Monograph No. 2. New York: Mayor's Committee on Management Survey of City of New York, 1952.

Rapkin, Chester, Louis Winnick, and David M. Blank. *Housing Market Analysis.* Washington, D.C.: United States Housing and Home Finance Agency, 1953.

Rolph, Earl R. *Theory of Fiscal Economics.* Berkeley: University of California Press, 1954.

Sacks, Seymour, and William F. Hellmuth, Jr. *Financing Government in a Metropolitan Area: The Cleveland Experience.* New York: Free Press of Glencoe, 1961.

Sigafoos, R.A. *The Municipal Income Tax: Its History and Problems.* Chicago: Public Administration Service, 1955.

Simon, Herbert A. *Fiscal Aspects of Metropolitan Consolidation.* Berkeley: University of California Press, 1943.

Simons, Henry C. *Federal Tax Reform*. Chicago: University of Chicago Press, 1950.

Stocker, Frederick D. *Nonproperty Taxes as Sources of Local Revenue*. Bulletin 903. Ithaca, New York: Cornell University Agricultural Experiment Station, December 1953.

Sundelson, J.W., and S.J. Mushkin. *The Measurement of State and Local Tax Effort*. Washington, D.C.: Social Security Board, 1944.

Tax Foundation, Inc.
City Income Taxes. New York: December 1967.

Fiscal Outlook for State and Local Government to 1975. New York: 1966.

Tax Burdens and Benefits of Government Expenditures by Income Class, 1961 and 1965. New York: 1967.

Tax Institute of America.
The Property Tax: Problems and Potentials. Princeton: 1967.

State and Local Taxes on Business. Princeton: 1965.

Taylor, Milton C.
Local Income Taxes as a Source of Revenue for Michigan Cities. East Lansing: Michigan State University, 1961.

Michigan City Income Tax Reform. East Lansing: Institute for Community Development and Services, Michigan State University, 1969.

Turvey, Ralph. *The Economics of Real Property*. London: George Allen and Unwin, 1957.

Vickrey, William. *Agenda for Progressive Taxation*. New York: Ronald Press, 1947.

Vieg, J.A., et al. *California Local Finance.* Stanford: Stanford University Press, 1960.

von Mering, Otto. *The Shifting and Incidence of Taxation.* Philadelphia: The Blakiston Company, 1942.

University of Wisconsin Tax Study Committee. *Wisconsin's State and Local Tax Burden: Impact, Incidence, and Tax Revision Alternatives.* Madison: 1959.

ARTICLES

Andrews, Richard B.
"Mechanics of the Urban Economic Base: The Problem of Terminology," *Land Economics*, 29(3): 263-268 (1953).

"Mechanics of the Urban Economic Base: A Classification of Base Types," *Land Economics*, 29(4): 343-350 (1953).

"Mechanics of the Urban Economic Base: The Problem of Base Measurement," *Land Economics*, 30(1): 52-60 (1954).

"Mechanics of the Urban Economic Base: General Problems of Base Identification," *Land Economics*, 30(2): 164-172 (1954).

"Mechanics of the Urban Economic Base: Special Problems of Base Identification," *Land Economics*, 30(3): 260-269 (1954).

"Mechanics of the Urban Economic Base: The Problem of Base Area Delimitation," *Land Economics*, 30(4): 309-319 (1954).

"Mechanics of the Urban Economic Base: The Base Concept and the Planning Process," *Land Economics*, 32(1): 69-84 (1956).

Bishop, George A. "The Tax Burden by Income-class, 1958," *National Tax Journal*, 14(1): 41-58 (1961).

Blank, David M., and Louis Winnick. "The Structure of the Housing Market," *Quarterly Journal of Economics*, 67(2): 181-208 (1953).

Blumenfeld, Hans. "The Economic Base of the Metropolis," *Journal of the American Institute of Planners*, 21(4): 114-132 (1955).

Brazer, Harvey E. "The Role of Major Metropolitan Centers in State and Local Finance," *American Economic Review*, 48(2): 305-317 (1958).

Brazer, Marjorie Cahn. "Economic and Social Disparities Between Central Cities and Their Suburbs," *Land Economics*, 43(3): 294-302 (1967).

Bronder, Leonard D. "Michigan's First Local Income Tax," *National Tax Journal*, 15(4): 423-431 (1962).

Brownlee, O.H.
"Estimated Distribution of Minnesota Taxes and Public Expenditure Benefits." In *Studies in Economics and Business No. 21*. Minneapolis: University of Minnesota Press, 1960.

"User Prices vs. Taxes" National Bureau of Economic Research, *Public Finances: Needs, Sources, and Utilization*. Princeton: Princeton University Press, 1961, 421-432.

Buehler, Alfred G.
"The Capitalization of Taxes," *National Tax Journal*, 3(4): 283-297 (1950).

"Problems Presented by Proliferation of Municipal Nonproperty Taxes," *Municipal Finance*, 34(3): 106-111 (1962).

Butters, J. Keith. "Taxation, Incentives, and Financial Capacity" in American Economic Association, *Readings in Fiscal Policy*. Homewood, Ill.: R.D. Irwin, 1955, 502-520.

Campbell, Alan K. "Taxes and Industrial Location in the New York Metropolitan Region," *National Tax Journal*, 11(3): 195-218 (1958).

Cheng, Pao L., and Alfred L. Edwards. "Compensatory Property Taxation: an Alternative," *National Tax Journal*, 12(3): 270-275 (1959).

Davies, David G.
"An Empirical Test on Sales-Tax Regressivity," *Journal of Political Economy*, 67(1): 72-78 (1959).

"The Relative Burden of Sales Taxation: A Statistical Analysis of California Data," *American Journal of Economics and Sociology*, 19(3): 289-296 (1960).

"The Sensitivity of Consumption Taxes to Fluctuations in Income," *National Tax Journal*, 15(3): 281-290 (1962).

Deran, Elizabeth. "Tax Structure in Cities Using the Income Tax," *National Tax Journal*, 21(2): 147-152 (1968).

Donheiser, Alan D. "The Incidence of the New York City Tax System" in *Financing Government in New York City*. Final Research Report to Temporary Commission on City Finances, City of New York. New York: Graduate School of Public Administration, New York University, 1966, 153-207.

Due, John F. "Local Non-Property Taxes: Effects on Economic Activity and Development," *Canadian Tax Journal*, 2(4): 228-234 (1954).

Ecker-Racz, L.L., and I.M. Labovitz. "Practical Solutions to Financial Problems Created by the Multilevel Political Structure" in National Bureau of Economic Research, *Public Finances: Needs, Sources, and Utilization*. Princeton: Princeton University Press, 1961, 135-221.

Fasiani, Mauro. "Materials for a Theory of the Duration of the Process of Tax Shifting," *The Review of Economic Studies*, 1(2): 81-101 (1934).

Feinberg, Mordecai S. "The Implications of Core-City Decline for the Fiscal Structure of the Core-City," *National Tax Journal*, 17(3): 213-231 (1964).

Fisher, Glenn W. "Determinants of State and Local Government Expenditures: A Preliminary Analysis," *National Tax Journal*, 14(4): 349-355 (1961).

Fitch, Lyle C. "Discussion," *American Economic Review*, 48(2): 328-330 (1958).

Grebler, Leo. "The Housing Inventory: Analytic Concepts and Quantitative Change," *American Economic Review*, 41(2): 555-568 (1951).

Hamovitch, William.
"Effects of Increases in Sales Tax Rates on Taxable Sales in New York City" in *Financing Government in New York City*. Final Research Report to Temporary Commission on City Finances, City of New York. New York: Graduate School of Public Administration, New York University, 1966, 619-633.

"Sales Taxation: An Analysis of the Effects of Rate Increases in Two Contrasting Cases," *National Tax Journal*, 19(4): 411-420 (1966).

Hansen, Reed R. "An Empirical Analysis of the Retail Sales Tax with Policy Recommendations," *National Tax Journal*, 15(1): 1-13 (1962).

Hawley, Amos H. "Metropolitan Population and Municipal Government Expenditures in Central Cities," *Journal of Social Issues*, 7(1,2): 100-108 (1951).

Homuth, H.G. "The Taxpayer Angle on Local Income Tax Administration" in *Income Tax Administration*. New York: Tax Institute, Inc., 1949, 329-349.

Januta, Donatas. "The Municipal Revenue Crisis: California Problems and Possibilities." 56 *California Law Review* 6: 1525-1558 (1968).

Jensen, Jens.P. "Tax Capitalization," *The Bulletin of the National Tax Association*, 23: 45-56 (November 1937).

Kee, Woo Sik.
"Central City Expenditures and Metropolitan Areas," *National Tax Journal*, 18(4): 337-353 (1965).

"City-Suburban Differentials in Local Government Fiscal Effort," *National Tax Journal*, 21(2): 183-189 (1968).

"Suburban Population Growth and its Implications for Core City Finance," *Land Economics*, 43(2): 202-211 (1967).

Klaman, Saul B. "Effects of Credit and Monetary Policy on Real Estate Markets: 1952-54," *Land Economics*, 32(3): 239-249 (1956).

Kressbach, Thomas W. "Local Income Taxation: A Comparative Analysis," *Michigan Municipal Review*, 37(7): 161-165 (1964).

Kurtzman, D.H. "Local Income Tax Administration in Pennsylvania" in *Income Tax Administration*. New York: Tax Institute, Inc., 1949, 305-318.

Leland, Simeon E. "An Ideal Theoretical Plan of Finance for a Metropolitan Area" in *Financing Metropolitan Government*. Princeton: Tax Institute, Inc., 1955, 233-270.

Levin, Henry M. "An Analysis of the Economic Effects of the New York City Sales Tax" in *Financing Government in New York City*. Final Research Report to Temporary Commission on City Finances, City of New York. New York: Graduate School of Public Administration, New York University, 1966, 635-691.

Lynn, Arthur D., Jr. "Local Income Taxation in the United States with Special Reference to the State of Ohio," *Journal of Finance*, 11(1): 80-82 (1956).

Maisel, Sherman J.
"Nonbusiness Construction," in J.S. Duesenberry, et al., eds., *The Brookings Quarterly Econometric Model of the United States*. Chicago: Rand McNally and Company, 1965.

"The Relationship of Residential Financing and Expenditures on Residential Construction," in United States Savings and Loan League, *Proceedings of the Conference on Savings and Residential Financing* (1965), 129-151.

"A Theory of Fluctuations in Residential Construction Starts," *American Economic Review*, 53(3): 359-383 (1963).

Maisel, Sherman J., and Leo Grebler. "Determinants of Residential Construction: A Review of Present Knowledge," in Commission on Money and Credit, *Impacts of Monetary Policy*. Englewood Cliffs, N.J.: Prentice-Hall, 1963, 475-620.

Margolis, Julius.
"Metropolitan Finance Problems: Territories, Functions, and Growth" in National Bureau of Economic Research, *Public Finances: Needs, Sources, and Utilization*. Princeton: Princeton University Press, 1961, 229-270.

"Municipal Fiscal Structure in a Metropolitan Region," *Journal of Political Economy*, 65(3): 225-236 (1957).

"The Variation of Property Tax Rates within a Metropolitan Region," *National Tax Journal*, 9(4): 326-330 (1956).

McLure, Charles E., Jr.
"Commodity Tax Incidence in Open Economies," *National Tax Journal*, 17(2): 187-204 (1964).

McLure, Charles E., Jr.
  "Tax Exporting in the United States: Estimates for
  1962," *National Tax Journal*, 20(1): 49-77 (1967).

*The Municipal Income Tax. Proceedings of the Academy of
  Political Science*, 28(4) (1968).

Pfouts, R.W. "An Empirical Testing of the Economic Base
  Theory," *Journal of the American Institute of Planners*,
  23(2): 64-69 (1957).

Phillips, Jewell Cass. "Philadelphia's Income Tax After
  Twenty Years," *National Tax Journal*, 11(3): 241-253
  (1958).

Recht, Richard J., and Louis K. Loewenstein. "Variations in Rates of Return," *The Appraisal Journal*,
  33(2): 243-248 (1965).

Rolph, Earl R. "Interregional Trade and State Excise
  Taxes," *National Tax Journal*, 8(4): 388-392 (1955).

Salyzyn, Vladimir. "The Municipal Income Tax," *Municipal Finance*, 37(4): 169-172 (1965).

Sazama, Gerald W. "Equalization of Property Taxes for
  the Nation's Largest Central Cities," *National Tax
  Journal*, 18(2): 151-161 (1965).

Sears, G. Alden. "Incidence Profiles of a Real Estate
  Tax and Earned Income Tax: A Study in the Formal,
  Differential Incidence of Selected Local Taxes,"
  National Tax Journal, 17(4): 340-356 (1964).

Shoup, Carl S.
  "Capitalization and Shifting of the Property Tax" in
  Property Taxes. New York: Tax Policy League, Inc.,
  1940, 187-201.

"New York City's Financial Situation and the Transit
  Fare," *National Tax Journal*, 5(3): 218-226 (1952).

Sigafoos, R.A.
"Economic Aspects of Local Nonproperty Taxes on Business" in National Tax Association, *Proceedings of the Annual Conference on Taxation* (1960), 447-451.

"The Municipal Income Tax--A Janus in Disguise," *National Tax Journal*, 6(2): 188-193 (1953).

Spengler, Edwin H. "The Property Tax as a Benefit Tax" in *Property Taxes*. New York: Tax Policy League, Inc., 1940, 165-173.

Stockfisch, J.A.
"Fees and Service Charges as a Source of City Revenues: A Case Study of Los Angeles," *National Tax Journal*, 13(2): 97-121 (1960).

"On the Obsolescence of Incidence," *Public Finance*, 14(2): 125-148 (1959).

Taylor, Milton C. "Local Income Taxes After Twenty-One Years," *National Tax Journal*, 15(2): 113-124 (1962).

Townsend, Roswell G. "Inequalities of Residential Property Taxation in Metropolitan Boston," *National Tax Journal*, 4(4): 361-369 (1951).

Walker, Mabel. "The Inevitability of City Income Taxes," *Tax Policy*, 34(4,5): 3-12 (1967).

Warren, Albert L. "Detroit's First Year's Experience with the City Income Tax" in National Tax Association, *Proceedings of the Annual Conference on Taxation* (1963), 442-449.

Wessel, Robert H. "Cincinnati's Income Tax--an Emergency Financing Device," *National Tax Journal*, 9(1): 84-90 (1956).

White, Melvin, and Ann White.
"Horizontal Inequality in the Federal Tax Treatment of Homeowners and Tenants," *National Tax Journal*, 18(3): 225-239 (1965).

"A Personal Income Tax for New York City: Equity and Economic Effects" in *Financing Government in New York City*. Final Research Report to Temporary Commission on City Finances, City of New York. New York: Graduate School of Public Administration, New York University, 1966, 449-491.

Wicks, John H., and Michael N. Killworth. "Administrative and Compliance Costs of State and Local Taxes," *National Tax Journal*, 20(3): 309-315 (1967).

Wicks, John H., Robert A. Little, and Ralph A. Beck. "A Note on Capitalization of Property Tax Changes," *National Tax Journal*, 21(3): 263-265 (1968).

Williamson, K.M. "The Taxation of Real Estate: Survey of Recent Discussion," *Quarterly Journal of Economics*, 48(1): 96-128 (1933).

Woodard, F.O., and Ronald W. Brady. "Inductive Evidence of Tax Capitalization," *National Tax Journal*, 18(2): 193-201 (1965).

Zimmer, Basil G. "Differential Property Taxation in a Metropolitan Area," *National Tax Journal*, 11(3): 280-286 (1958).

OTHER SOURCES

Burch, Kenneth M. Director, Economic Development, Greater Cincinnati Chamber of Commerce, Cincinnati, Ohio. Letter written April 23, 1968.

Daicoff, Darwin W. "Capitalization of the Property Tax." Unpublished Ph.D. dissertation, Department of Economics, University of Michigan, 1961.

Davis, Frances E. Deputy Treasurer, City of Warren, Ohio. Letter written April 23, 1968.

Fahey, J.R. "The Advisability and Probable Effects of a Local Income or Local Sales Tax in Boston." Unpublished Ph.D. dissertation, Department of Economics, Massachusetts Institute of Technology, 1967.

Gillespie, Roy D. Executive Vice President of Lexington Chamber of Commerce, Lexington, Kentucky. Letter written April 19, 1968.

Harb, Richard K. Manager, Research Department, Louisville Chamber of Commerce, Louisville, Kentucky. Letter written April 15, 1968.

Laubscher, Harold R. Manager, Gadsden Chamber of Commerce, Gadsden, Alabama. Letter written April 19, 1968.

Maine, Richard E. Letter written for Charles L. Benton, Director of Finance, Baltimore, Maryland, March 4, 1969.